RE-CONSTITUTION

HOW AMERICA CAN FINALLY BECOME A DEMOCRACY

by

Don Bacon

This brief work outlines a replacement for our existing Constitution, in the event of a future constitutional convention.

Copyright © 2020
All Rights Reserved

TABLE OF CONTENTS

Introduction   4

Pre-Constitution   7
- Government
- Laws
- Civil Rights
- Autonomy and Freedom
- Agency
- Democracy

Re-Constitution Text   20

Re-Constitution Explication   41
- Preamble
- Article I: Citizenship
- Article II: Branches and Levels of Government
- Article III: Enumeration of Civil Liberties and Rights
- Article IV: Federal Legislature
- Article V: Federal Executive
- Article VI: Federal Judiciary
- Article VII: The States
- Article VIII: Conduct of Elections
- Article IX: Citizens' Power of Referendum
- Article X: Citizens' Power of Ratification
- Article XI: Citizens' Power of Amendment

Afterword: Sweepings from the Cutting Room Floor   127

Appendix: Constitution Text   132

Essays on Government   162
- The 4th Amendment vs. The Surveillance State

- Do Public Officials Have Fiduciary Obligations to Us?
- Money in Politics: Why We Are Where We Are
- Campaign Contributions: Foreign, Anonymous, Nefarious?
- Neutralizing the Influence of Money Over Politics
- How America Could Become a Democracy
- How Much Democracy Do We Have? How Much Do We Want?
- What Real Health Care Reform Might Look Like
- Obamacare: Pragmatism vs. Principle
- The Federal Government Lacks Constitutional Authority to Use Taxation to Regulate Behavior
- Can Government Require Us to Purchase Health Insurance?
- A Requirement to Marry, the Constitution, and the Individual Mandate

Introduction

Our Constitution is arguably the greatest political document ever written. The role and organization of government it describes has provided a framework for the phenomenal success of the United States, making the work of a few dozen men in the hot Philadelphia summer of 1787 a quantum leap forward in human history.

So why rewrite it, and reorganize our government and society, if the Constitution has served us so well?

Because at this advanced stage of our history, we can ensure a more secure future for ourselves and our country if the principles of the Constitution are redrafted and updated in a modern document that is clearer, more consistent, less prey to misinterpretation, and where frankly, a number of archaic constitutional relics are eliminated. While our Constitution's sturdy longevity would no doubt gratify the Framers, it was written for a nation that has changed almost beyond recognition over the centuries.

One change the Framers would note today is our reverence and desire for democracy, a regard most of them didn't share and that is generally absent from our Constitution. A central tenet of this work is that we do not now enjoy – and cannot in the future achieve – a genuine American democracy without a major constitutional overhaul. The Framers, it is contended, would readily agree that to shape a thoroughgoing democracy within our current Constitution is to fit a round peg into a square hole, because democracy is not what they intended or even mentioned. We have been living through decades of awkward constitutional whittling as a result.

Within a true democracy, our Constitution would be a fundamental social contract between all Americans, a contemporary agreement as to how we choose to govern ourselves as a nation. Our Constitution bears scant resemblance to a democratic social contract: its outdated language is easy to twist, and many of the purposes the Constitution addresses are no longer relevant or even laudable. A slew of new issues has arisen that the Framers could not possibly have envisioned, for which our Constitution provides little or no direction.

Libraries are filled with books that marvel at the Constitution's groundbreaking brilliance, while detailing its ambiguities, contradictions and failings, familiar territory which this volume will avoid retreading unless necessary. It is a truism that 21st century America lacks the direction and mission we evinced for our first two hundred years. References to the American Century are in the past tense, yet our best days can still lie ahead. That will not happen unless we bluntly diagnose ourselves as a nation in a midlife malaise. A Re-Constitution, that restates and reinvigorates our principles, while taking a new quantum leap toward the world's first genuinely democratic republic, offers the prospect of a new lease on the American experiment, and more centuries of progress.

For those readers who disagree, and believe our Constitution serves us perfectly well as it is written, the author's request is that skeptics read through this guide with an open mind, to see if in fact problematic constitutional issues are rightly exposed and improved replacement language provided. The only possible proof of the updated constitutional pudding proposed below is in the reading.

The format of this book will first present the complete text of the proposed Re-Constitution, to provide a read-through and an overall sense of the document's direction. Following chapters will then explicate the text, comparing it with corresponding language in our existing Constitution, a copy of which is included in an appendix. To conclude, a dozen essays on government are reissued as background material.

Before we embark on a constitutional rewrite, we should briefly discuss the principles underlying our notions of government, law, civil rights and democracy.

Pre-Constitution

Government

A good starting point is to ask ourselves some very basic questions about what government is, what are its origins, and fundamentally what it means to govern someone or something.

Revolutionary Poetic License

The Declaration of Independence offers an explanation of the origin of government in its first sentences, holding it to be self-evidently true that:

> all men are created equal, that they are endowed by their Creator with certain unalienable rights, that among these are life, liberty and the pursuit of happiness. That to secure these rights, governments are instituted among men, deriving their just powers from the consent of the governed.

The idea here is that humans have certain fundamental rights, and that "governments are instituted among men" in order to "secure these rights." In other words, the purpose of government, and the reason it is brought into existence, and derives any justification for its continued existence, is to secure and protect pre-existing rights of individuals.

While the authors had a more immediate purpose in writing the Declaration – to justify an attempted secession from the dominant empire of the epoch – than articulating a theory of the origin of government, the explanation they offered is nonetheless self-evidently *not* true. Governments have not as a rule come into being by public consent, in order to protect the rights of those governed. That is the type of government the Founders may have *wanted* to institute, but there have been relatively few governments throughout history that would even approximate their description. 'Government' from its earliest glimmerings probably amounted to one or more individuals within a group of humans controlling the actions of the rest, to a greater or lesser degree. Even to this day, sheer dominance of the few over the many continues to be the unfortunate norm.

Animal Government

Humans didn't invent government, per se. We inherited it from animals that live in groups. Primates and canines and many other types of animals have rudimentary government expressed through the dominance of one or more individuals within a social group. The alphas, usually through physical superiority, control the behavior of lessers within the social group. The control and dominance can have evolutionary purpose, for example organizing a social group into a more effective collective hunting force, or enforcing mating relations, or parceling scarce food resources. Primitive government exists within animal groups, normally where the physically dominant are self-appointed leaders who control and dictate the actions and behavior of their lessers within the social group.

Hominid Government

It may never be possible to pinpoint the prevalent social forms of our primeval ancestors, the early hominids, who comprised a number of species spanning millions of years. The safest assumption is that they grew out of higher primate social structures, which exhibit elaborate dominance relations within their groupings.

Above all, hominids needed to protect themselves from predators, both animals and other hominids, using any survival technique available. In these earliest stages of development, the most physically powerful individuals provided indispensable protection, resources and cohesion to a grouping, while enjoying the prerogatives of dominance. This, we shall assume without direct evidence, was the kernel of hominid government: largely a carryover from primates, where a necessary dominance and control of one or more leaders functioned to ensure group survival.

Human Government

Nevertheless every hominid species eventually became extinct, but one. Modern archaeology and anthropology have been steadily amassing evidence that *homo sapiens* succeeded where all others failed, by evolving an amazing adaptive versatility. The more we learn about early human social development, the more variety we discover in different societies' responses to the circumstances facing them. Even when different social groupings faced similar challenges, they often chose starkly different paths to survival and success.

From our prehistory down to modern times, the human capacity for adaptive versatility has allowed us in some societies to depart from animal-derived social structures dominated by the physically powerful. While other-imposed, top-down government has certainly been the norm, humanity has also proven itself capable – through communication and collective cooperation – of creating forms of government that distribute power and decision-making. Our existing Constitution is a sterling example of humanity's capacity for political innovation.

Laws

The origin and purpose of laws can be discerned by returning to the paradigm of early hominid groups, where one or more individuals are assumed to have dominated and controlled the actions of the remainder. That is to say, the dominant enforced *rules* of behavior – dos and don'ts – on those they controlled, through physical coercion or other punishments, such as shunning or ostracism. As we progressed, a human grouping – or parts of it – may in many instances have played a widening role in creating its social order. In any case, those rules – however derived – over time become engrained as *customs* within a society.

Laws by historical extension arose as the formalized, codified rules that in most cases the dominant impose on the remainder of the population to control behavior and stabilize and perpetuate their social dominance. It is not surprising that the first written legal codes we find throughout ancient history, such as the Code of Hammurabi, were developed in the Fertile Crescent by newly sedentary agricultural societies that needed increased cooperation, discipline and institutional order to both fend off external invasion and enhance internal controls over an expanding population. The importance of property within the new social order was reflected by a plethora of laws governing theft, trade, borrowing, and increasingly refined notions of ownership.

Civil Rights

Much ink has been spilled over the nature and origin of human or civil rights (and civil liberties, a closely related concept), but the various theories usually fall into one of three schools of thought.

God-Given Rights

The first school is clearly articulated by the Declaration of Independence, where "...men...are endowed by their Creator with certain unalienable rights...." In other words, God gave us certain rights, so fundamental and unalienable that we always possess these rights, even if circumstances are such that we cannot protect and exercise our rights. So that a slave has the same unalienable rights as a free person, the key difference being that as a slave the rights are not in that circumstance exercisable. But they still exist, unalienable.

The problem with that explanation of the origin of civil rights is that God may not in fact exist, or at any rate the existence of God may not be provable; and in any case if God does exist, He or She may not care a fig for human rights, and have bothered to endow us with any. The argument fails because it presumes to build the edifice of rights on a foundation that is not provable, may not exist, and is therefore conjecture.

'Natural Rights'

Nevertheless the notion that our human or civil rights are inherent within ourselves, that is, essential and necessary to our existence, is very attractive. So an alternative school of rights arose, that tried to establish their existence without reference to God. There are a few variants to this theory, but most assert in one guise or another that we possess 'natural rights' as essential elements of our 'human nature.' Unfortunately theories of natural rights share the same embarrassing defect as any theistic theory of rights: they lack provable foundation. They boil down to assertions.

Proponents of natural rights theory are understandably often keen to avoid or deny its reliance on the existence of a human nature, for which we have no evidence. It is true that humans have certain characteristics that distinguish us from other animals; but an 'essence' or 'nature' within which our rights are embedded?

Science points in the opposite direction, to a human species that is undergoing constant evolution, like all living creatures. If we evolved from the simplest forms of life, at what point (and why, and how) did we acquire 'natural rights' and a 'human nature'? And if pond scum doesn't have natural rights, but we now do as sufficiently evolved human beings, couldn't we (or some of us) *devolve* back into something primitive enough to no longer have natural rights or a human nature?

Rights as Government Grants

The third camp dispenses with reliance on God, or an Aristotelian human nature, and instead posits that rights exist if and only if government grants them to us. Under this scenario, rights are not inherent and unalienable. Quite the contrary, they are creations of government, grants that can be taken away just as they are given. Under this theory rights are not recognized by government, they are created by government. They are understood to be a construct of human progress, which is one of the stronger arguments for this way of thinking: formal recognition of human and civil rights has developed organically through history, by the actions of governments. To this day, a person in one country may enjoy a civil right; cross a foreign border, and that right might disappear.

The problem with what is sometimes known as the positivist school of human rights is that it preserves no real distinction between rights and privileges. If a right can be here today, gone tomorrow, or not even exist in a neighboring country, how is that civil right different from a privilege, which can be revoked by governing authority at any time?

It should be noted that the God theory of rights has the same problem. What if God decides to revoke the right He or She endowed you with? We are talking about God here, Who can change His or Her Mind without our approval. Whether a right is granted by God or Government, it would seem to be revocable, and therefore anything but unalienable.

The popular theories of the origin of civil rights – whether God-endowed, by 'natural right,' or government grant – end up sinking in the same intellectual morass. Yet most of us believe that we all do indeed possess certain basic human rights. Let's find a rights situation that reasonable people can agree upon, and build from there.

Autonomy and Freedom

Imagine that you are somewhere minding your own business, and are assaulted by someone without warning. You don't know your assailant's intentions: he or she may be trying to kill you, or injure you, or abduct you.

No reasonable person can disagree that you have the right to defend yourself. No reasonable person can disagree that in the course of protecting yourself from injury, or abduction, or death, *if your intention is simply to protect yourself*, you might injure or even kill your assailant, and yet be held blameless. Your purpose is merely to defend yourself, and if harm (even death) comes to your assailant as a result of your defense, you have done no more than exercise your *right* to self-defense.

Not only do we recognize a right of self-defense for ourselves, we extend the same recognition to the animal world. If an animal in the wild is attacked by another, and successfully defends itself, even to the point of killing its assailant, we do not find fault. If we take a dog for a walk, and it defends itself from attack by another dog, we assign no fault: clearly all animals, including humans, have the right to defend themselves from physical harm.

While this truth is unquestionable, it is not so clear why. What concept underlies our recognition that self-defense is a universal right?

Arena of Autonomy

It would be difficult to find any reasonable person who did not assume that as an individual, he or she has what will be called here an *arena of autonomy,* within which that person (and no one else) deserves control over their own life. Self-preservation – defending against anyone or anything that attempts to physically harm us – is only the most basic right we assume, without question, to possess within that arena of autonomy. Our collective understanding of the arena has steadily grown over the eons; in fact much of the march of history can be interpreted through the lens of society's ever-expanding notion of an individual's autonomous zone, where he or she is either free *to* do (or not do) something; or conversely, where an individual is free *from* having something done to him or her. Every right we recognize can be construed as a 'to' freedom and/or a 'from' freedom.

Mutuality of a Right/Freedom

A *right* is further defined here as any freedom that an individual can have, such that exercise or enjoyment of that right does not impinge another individual's freedom of the same kind. In other words, a right/freedom only qualifies as such if it can be mutually shared by all individuals. A right/freedom can be included in one person's arena of autonomy, if and only if it can equally be included in all persons' respective arenas of autonomy.

By contrast, a *privilege* does not require mutuality: it can be enjoyed by some, and not others. Unlike a right/freedom, a privilege is a grant from one party to another, which can be modified or withdrawn by the grantor, or even rejected by the intended grantee.

Maximizing Mutual Arenas of Autonomy

The progress of history down the ages (with many detours) has been finding and maximizing a mutual arena of autonomy for individuals to exercise and enjoy rights/freedoms within a society. It is an ongoing zigzag process, at different stages in different societies across the planet, but human society in general has been heading in the direction of maximizing a mutually compatible arena of autonomy for individuals.

There are still places where a person's right to be physically free is unrecognized, but slavery and the slave trade, once ubiquitous, are increasingly rare, as are other forms of involuntary servitude. Much of the planet still does not recognize that persons should be free to choose their spouses, but arranged marriages are in decline. In the United States laws against interracial marriage survived deep into the twentieth century; same-sex marriage waited for the twenty-first century. Throughout most of history young adults coming of age could not freely choose an occupation. People are often still restricted from traveling or living where they wish, or even expressing their thoughts. The point is that on all these (and many other) rights issues, history is moving forward however painfully in the direction of maximizing a person's arena of autonomy.

Childhood: An Emerging Autonomy

Our largely unconscious understanding of human autonomy can also be seen in how we treat children. Clearly we do not see them from birth as autonomous creatures: it will be years before a child can grow to take care of itself and exercise autonomy. When it can, that is our definition of adulthood. Until then, the legal obligations of a parent or guardian are designed to protect and nurture the child while it matures into the autonomy of adulthood, recognizing that the child has a panoply of rights from its first breath. The life of a child as its rights/freedoms emerge is akin to a time-elapse film of the history of humankind, with the teenage years preceding adulthood resembling the age of revolutions.

Agency

The word *agency* will be used here to describe an individual's exercise of autonomy, that is, how one exercises rights/freedoms to do things, or refrain from doing things. It is an active concept, referring to what a person does or is capable of doing within their arena of autonomy, not to what happens to a person. Nor, in this discussion of rights/freedoms, will the concept of agency include actions a person has no right to commit, such as crime. In this context agency is defined more narrowly than the vernacular, only as a capacity to exercise rights/freedoms.

Agency by any definition admits of degree or range, even quantity. For example, we might see a mosquito as having a small degree of agency, while an eagle does more with its greater range of capabilities and thus can be said to have more agency. Agency is something that develops in an individual: a puppy may not be able to do much, but a trained dog can do many things, and thus in this parlance is considered to exercise greater agency. Childhood is one long process of developing agency, from at first simply being able to grab a finger, to attending school and in some cases changing the world.

While *agency* will be used as a word for exercising freedoms, or to borrow a phrase, expressing oneself, its use is not intended to take a philosophical position on whether we possess 'free will,' or instead are fully caused to act and think by forces beyond our control. That way lies madness. Instead, agency is here defined as the exercise of rights/freedoms within a person's arena of autonomy, with the unproved assumption that for any individual, the more agency one can develop, the better.

Agency = Pursuit of Happiness

In fact there is every appearance that the sensation of developing and expressing one's autonomy, of exercising one's agency, is what most of us experience in life as the pursuit of happiness. When Jefferson listed "life, liberty and the pursuit of happiness," a chain-link connection can be construed between the first, second and third rights: without life, there can be no liberty; and without liberty, there can be no pursuit of happiness. The pursuit of happiness is for our purposes the active exercise of liberty, or in the language used here, the exercise of agency within an arena of autonomy. Happiness itself results when we interpret the agency's exercise as successful.

Democracy

Our existing Constitution was not written by authors overly fond of *democracy*, which will be defined as a system of government where all persons share the same political arena of autonomy, with the same *potential* political agency, whether they exercise it or not. James Madison called it 'mobocracy,' a state of affairs greatly to be feared. Not all Framers shared this opinion, but the majority did evince a palpable aversion to giving too much authority and responsibility to the general public. Every State had different voting qualifications, but generally the franchise was not extended to women, slaves, freedmen, Native Americans, or white men without sufficient property or wealth. Senators were chosen by State legislatures, not the public. The notion of 'one person, one vote' was often observed in the breach. Citizens residing in the District of Columbia were (and remain) unrepresented in Congress. And the Electoral College provided another buffer against the popular will, as necessary.

Most of these and other undemocratic provisions have been corrected by constitutional amendment, or softened by statute or judicial rulings or custom. It is undeniable – the Framers' intentions notwithstanding – that we have been moving inexorably in the direction of a democratic society. Why are we so attracted to a form of government that our Framers actively avoided?

Democracy = Mutual Political Arena of Autonomy

The answer lies in the progress of modern society: today, every reasonable person's assumption, however unconscious, is that people should have control over their own lives, as much as mutually possible. Human capability has steadily developed and expanded throughout history, providing society a direction, which in most cases has been toward a public recognition of an individual's widening rights, that is, a growing shared arena of autonomy wherein a person can enjoy ever greater rights/freedoms, and exercise ever greater agency. On repeated occasions that has translated into a desire for ever greater *political* agency, with the goal of a society where all persons have a roughly equal potential say (i.e., agency) in the running of their nation, state, and locality. The modern understanding is that a person cannot be said to truly have control over his or her own life – to be free – if that person does not share an arena of political rights/freedoms with all others, to participate as political equals in government, if that person chooses to do so.

History's Directionality Toward Democracy

By embracing the fact that our history has demonstrated this mutually beneficial directionality, democracy is accepted here – certainly not as inevitable, but without argument as a consensus Good to be pursued and maximized. While government largely remains as it began – a tool for the powerful to dominate a population – a vast majority clearly has the desire at this stage of history to institute a government where all persons enjoy the same political rights/freedoms, the same shared arena of autonomy, within which they can exercise the same political agency, if they choose.

As Americans, most of us are convinced of the rightness and desirability of democracy; our existing Constitution, properly interpreted, even extensively amended, is not. For decades we have been struggling in the direction of the type of government the Founders imagined in the 1776 Declaration of Independence – one instituted by the consent of the governed, for the protection of their rights – in other words, a democracy. No wonder it is such slow sledding: the Framers gave us a 1787 Constitution designed to guard against that very outcome.

THE RE-CONSTITUTION OF THE UNITED STATES OF AMERICA

Preamble

We the Citizens of the United States of America, in order to perfect our representative democracy—a government intended to be of, by, and for the citizens of this republic—do hereby replace our Constitution and its amendments with this Re-Constitution, expanding the civil liberties and rights of all persons and improving the federalism by which the Union is preserved and protected.

Article I Citizenship

A **natural-born citizen** of the United States shall be anyone who, at the time of his or her birth, has a biological parent who is a citizen. A **naturalized citizen** shall be anyone who fulfills the legal requirements of naturalization as established by Congress. Citizens eighteen years of age or older may vote in elections, and shall be eligible to serve in public office and on juries. Citizenship and its benefits shall be privileges, revocable for just cause by due process in a federal court of law.

Article II Branches and Levels of Government

The government of the United States shall be separated into three branches—**legislative, executive, and judicial**—in order that the branches check and balance one another's powers. Our government shall also be separated into three levels—**federal, state, and local**. Federal authority and law shall extend to all matters between or shared by the States, all matters external to the United States, and the District of

Columbia. A State's authority and law shall extend to all matters internal to that State, which shall divide itself into political subdivisions, in order that local authority and law extend to all matters specific to the different locales. Wherever reasonable alternatives exist, government shall not practice commerce. This Re-Constitution, its amendments, and all federal laws and treaties in conformity with this Re-Constitution, shall be the supreme law of the land, to which all branches and levels of government shall conform their laws and actions. The proceedings of government shall be conducted in public wherever possible, with thorough and accurate records freely available.

Article III Enumeration of Civil Liberties and Rights

Persons apprehended making war against the United States, or assisting in the furtherance thereof, shall be subject to military law and justice. For all other persons, the protection of the following civil liberties and rights shall be guaranteed by all branches and levels of government within the States, the District of Columbia, and all territories and possessions of the United States:

1. **Freedom from slavery and involuntary servitude.**

2. **Freedom from discrimination**, for reason of race, ethnicity, national origin, religion, gender, sexual orientation, age, disability, degree of wealth, opinion, residency, or manner of living. All persons shall receive equal protection of the laws.

3. **Freedom of expression** in all subjects, communicated or created in any medium or manner, public and private. Persons shall be liable for their expression, if in violation of another's civil liberties, rights, or other protections provided in law.

4. **Freedom of association** and organization for any peaceful purpose, including the right to assemble, protest and petition the government for a redress of grievances, and to travel freely within the States, the District of Columbia, and all territories and possessions of the United States.

5. **Right of self-protection**, to defend one's own and others' safety from bodily harm, to keep arms for personal protection in one's domicile, and to bear arms in defense of the United States against tyranny, insurrection or invasion.

6. **Right of emergency medical treatment**, for all persons from any medical facility, regardless of ability to pay, in the event of a life-threatening emergency or catastrophe, manmade or natural.

7. **Freedom from government taking of private property**, unless after due process of law the property shall be owned by the public for its use, and unless the owner is compensated at fair market value for the property taken. The original owner or designated heir(s) shall have first right of refusal to purchase the property at fair market value if it is offered for private ownership in the future.

8. **Right to shelter, and freedom from vagrancy**. To preserve public health and safety, government shall provide shelter and assistance for the indigent as necessary, and prohibit vagrancy.

9. **Rights of privacy**:

A. To be secure upon private property from searches and seizures unless with written warrant, issued by the court of jurisdiction to law enforcement authorities after presentation under oath of substantial evidence of probable wrongdoing, and which defines the limits of the search and persons or things to be seized. In public, persons and personal property are subject to non-warranted search and seizure only under exigent circumstances and upon evidence of probable wrongdoing, or as a security precaution before entering a public space. Absent a compelling interest, government shall not constrain persons' conduct of their private lives.

B. Whatever information the public cannot lawfully learn about a person without his or her permission, the government shall not acquire without a court warrant. Any information that a business or organization acquires about a person, as a result of the person using or communicating with the business or organization, shall not be divulged to any third party without that person's consent, unless ordered to do so by court warrant. Consent shall be in writing, and specify the information the business or organization wishes to divulge, the desired recipient(s), and the reason(s) for wishing to do so.

10. **Rights upon criminal arrest and trial**:

A. To be informed of one's legal rights at the time of arrest, including the right to due process of law, to remain silent before law enforcement authorities, and to a competent attorney, court-appointed if requested.

B. To a writ of habeas corpus, namely, to promptly appear before the court of jurisdiction and hear legitimate causes for one's arrest, and the exact accusation, or be freed. The accused shall not be presented in court, nor otherwise displayed in public, wearing prison garb or physical restraints. The accused shall be subject to trial only upon presentation of sufficient prima facie proof to the court of jurisdiction, that if unrebutted, would demonstrate guilt. Criminal grand juries are prohibited. No person shall be held captive or detained without charge, or in order to prevent the potential commission of a crime.

C. To humane treatment in government custody, and to be released on personal recognizance pending trial, unless there is compelling evidence that the accused is dangerous or a flight risk. In that event, the accused shall remain incarcerated pending expedited trial. Bail is prohibited.

D. To a timely and public trial, on specific and self-consistent charges, heard by an impartial jury of one's peers, on the principle that the accused is to be found innocent unless proven guilty beyond a reasonable doubt by unanimous verdict of the jurors. Persons accused of crimes allegedly committed before the age of eighteen shall be tried as juveniles.

E. To full prior discovery and examination of all evidence for the prosecution, to hear and cross-examine witnesses for the prosecution, and to use the authority of the court to subpoena witnesses in one's defense. No persons shall be allowed to testify in any criminal or civil trial who have received or been promised benefit in return for their testimony, with the following exception. Upon written request by any principal in any criminal or civil trial, the court shall subpoena impartial expert witnesses to testify without being informed who requested the expert opinions, and shall compensate the experts at a rate sufficient to encourage their service.

F. To decline to testify, either for or against oneself, without implication of guilt. No person shall be required by government to incriminate or bring infamy upon oneself.

G. In the event of acquittal, to be free from future criminal retrial or civil trial, for the same alleged offense.

H. In the event of conviction, freedom from penalties that include unreasonable fines or cruel punishments; and the right to appeal one's conviction on procedural, factual, and legal grounds.

11. **Right to due process and an impartial jury of one's peers in civil trials**, whether plaintiff or defendant. To achieve legal standing, plaintiffs must make an arguable prima facie demonstration that they are or have been damaged by the defendant.

12. **Right of equal opportunity for legal justice.** In order that a person's degree of wealth not prejudice his or her access to or results within the legal system, attorneys at law shall be publicly reimbursed for time spent and reasonable expenses in criminal defense, and in civil actions that the court of jurisdiction has found triable, with the following exceptions: their clients may choose private over public reimbursement; and clients who lose civil actions to any party other than a public agency shall be liable for private reimbursement of attorneys for plaintiff and defendant. Government shall maintain rates of reimbursement sufficient to encourage competent attorneys to represent persons who choose public funding. Government shall not seize, hold, sequester, or effect the forfeiture of persons' assets unless as specified within a judicial judgment beyond appeal.

13. **Freedom from *ex post facto* laws, and government intrusion in private contracts**. The lawfulness of an action, contract, or state of affairs shall be preserved in accordance with the laws in place at the time the action was committed, the contract executed, or the state of affairs first obtained. Government shall not abrogate, nullify, or modify a legal, written contract between consenting parties, nor require persons to enter into contracts.

14. **Freedom from subpoena to appear before any legislative body, or from questioning by any law enforcement or executive agency.** Only judicial authority may subpoena witnesses, or require an oath or affirmation of truthfulness, or penalize any failure to appear or speak truthfully. It shall not be a crime to be untruthful to any legislative body or law enforcement or executive agency.

15. **Compensation for damages incurred by criminal investigations that do not result in charges, trials that do not result in convictions, or convictions that are overturned.** If a person suffers damages or losses as a result of criminal investigation in which the person is not charged, or as a result of a trial in which the person is not convicted, or as a result of a conviction that is overturned on appeal, that person may present to the court of jurisdiction evidence of the damages or losses, and the court shall reward compensation from public funds for the entirety of the damages or losses.

Article IV Federal Legislature

The bicameral **Congress of the United States**, consisting of the **Senate** and the **House of Representatives**, shall be the federal legislative authority. It shall have sole powers to originate and vote upon all proposals, including all bills proposed to become law, for all matters between or shared by the States, external to the United States, and the District of Columbia.

Section 1 Any candidate for **Senator** or **Representative** must be at least twenty-five years of age on the day of election, and have been a citizen of the United States for seven years, and a resident of the State or congressional district for one year. Senators and Representatives shall be elected for a term of four years, and shall be limited to no more than two consecutive terms. After one term out of their previous office,

Senators or Representatives shall become eligible to return to their respective chamber. In the first election after ratification of this Re-Constitution, all positions for Senator and Representative shall be balloted and filled. One newly elected Senator from each State, and the closest approximation to one half of the newly elected Representatives from each State and the District of Columbia, except those from States or the District of Columbia with only one Representative, shall be randomly selected after the results of the election are final to serve for a two-year term. Those Senators and Representatives serving the initial two-year term may afterward seek re-election for two consecutive four-year terms in their respective chamber.

Section 2 The Senate shall consist of one hundred Senators, two from each State. Every two years, each State shall hold a state-wide election for one of its two senatorial positions. The House of Representatives shall consist of four hundred Representatives, apportioned to the States and the District of Columbia according to their number of citizens, as determined by a national census conducted every new decade. The decennial national census shall also determine each State's and the District of Columbia's total population, according to which Congress shall distribute federal costs and benefits.

Section 3 Congressional apportionment shall ensure that each Representative represents a congressional district of approximately the same number of citizens, except that every State and the District of Columbia shall be apportioned at least one Representative. Each State and the District of Columbia shall create congressional districts equal in number to its apportioned number of Representatives. Every two years, each State and the District of Columbia shall hold elections for the House of Representatives in the closest approximation to one half of its congressional districts.

Section 4 Congress shall assemble in joint session on the first Monday of even-numbered months. Between joint sessions, the two chambers shall collaborate through a ten-member **Congressional Conference**, consisting of five Senators and five Representatives chosen by their respective chamber, who may replace its **Conferees** at will. The number of members of a political party assigned from a chamber to the Conference, or to any other joint or separate congressional committee, shall be proportionate to the percentage of party members within that chamber. Either chamber may meet separately at other times of its choosing, and may originate and vote upon any proposal, including a bill proposed to become law. Whether meeting in joint session or separately, if at least one half of the total number of Senators and one half of the total number of Representatives are in attendance, and if at least one half of those in attendance agree, any matter may be scheduled for a discussion and vote. In all sessions, votes of Senators and Representatives shall be conducted and counted separately, except when breaking a presidential election tie. Respective majorities and supermajorities shall be calculated based on each chamber's total number of members.

Section 5 A congressional proposal shall pertain to only one subject, and state the proposal's purpose as a preamble. Each federal appropriation shall be proposed separately. If any proposal is approved by one chamber, it shall be sent to the other chamber for consideration. If the proposal passes both chambers, whether in joint or separate sessions, it shall be presented to the President for executive approval. If the President approves, he or she shall sign the proposal and return it to Congress. If the President disapproves, within fourteen days he or she shall exercise a veto, by returning the unsigned proposal to Congress with objections. Congress, as it sees fit, may then reconsider the proposal in the light of the President's objections, either in joint or separate sessions, or both, and revote the proposal. If it is passed by Congress in joint session or by both chambers in separate sessions, upon agreement of two-thirds of Senators and two-thirds of Representatives, the proposal shall become law, or have the full force and effect of law. If the President does not return the proposal, signed or unsigned with objections, within fourteen days, the proposal shall become law, or have the full force and effect of law. Declarations of Congress nullifying an executive order are not subject to presidential veto.

Section 6 Either the Senate or the House of Representatives may impeach the President, Vice President, Justices of the Supreme Court and the High Court of Review, Judges of the lower federal courts, or federal executive branch department heads, if two-thirds of either Senators or Representatives agree. No more than one federal trial of impeachment may occur at any given time. Impeachments shall be tried in a special joint session of Congress, presided over by the Chief Justice of the Supreme Court when a President or Vice President is impeached, and by the Vice President for all other impeachment trials. The agreement of two-thirds of Senators and two-thirds of Representatives shall result in conviction and immediate removal of the convicted from office. Congress shall not impose further penalties or disabilities on any persons impeached and convicted, who are however subject to criminal law, while enjoying the same civil rights in the event of criminal arrest and prosecution as all other persons. Congress shall not conduct criminal prosecutions.

Section 7 The President and Vice President may not be concurrently impeached. If the President is impeached and convicted, the Vice President shall immediately succeed to the Presidency and appoint a new Vice President without the need for congressional approval. The office of the President shall at no time remain vacant. If the Vice President is impeached and convicted, the President shall appoint a new Vice President without the need for congressional approval. In either case, the

Vice Presidency shall be filled by the President within fourteen days. If not, Congress shall appoint a Vice President without delay.

Section 8 Senators and Representatives may not be removed from office by their respective chamber, nor may they be punished therein, except by censure. Senators and Representatives shall be removed from office either upon criminal felony conviction, or if they are recalled and replaced in a special election, as the different States may provide, if they see fit. Any vacancy in Congress by whatever cause shall be filled by the State from which the vacancy occurred, in the manner prescribed by that State's laws. As salary, Senators and Representatives shall receive three times the national average of gross ordinary income.

Section 9 The above provisions notwithstanding, the Senate and House of Representatives shall together make the rules by which they cooperate, and shall separately make the rules by which each chamber operates. The two chambers shall organize themselves into committees as they see fit and appoint their own officers, with the exception of the Vice President, who shall preside over Congress when meeting in joint session.

Article V Federal Executive

The **President** shall be the chief executive of the United States, and direct the federal executive authority, which shall be empowered and required to enact, administer, and enforce this Re-Constitution, its amendments, and the laws and actions approved by Congress.

Section 1 Any candidate for President must be at least thirty-five years of age on the day of election, and have been a citizen of the United States for the previous fourteen years.

The Presidency shall be determined by the voters of all the States and the District of Columbia, the winner to become the President, the runner-up to become the **Vice President**. In the event of a tie vote between candidates, the members of Congress in office at the time of the election shall choose between the tied candidates in special joint session, each Senator and Representative to have one vote. In the event of a tie vote in Congress, the Vice President at the time of the general election shall cast the deciding vote, but may not vote for him- or herself.

Section 2 Both the President and Vice President shall serve for the same term of four years. While the Vice President shall not be limited in the number of terms he or she may serve, the President may serve for no more than two terms. In the event that the President dies in office, or is determined by two-thirds of Senators and two-thirds of Representatives to be no longer able to serve due to mental or physical incapacity, the Vice President shall assume the Presidency for the remainder of the term of office, and within fourteen days shall appoint a new Vice President without the need for congressional approval. If not, Congress shall appoint a Vice President without delay. Any Vice President assuming the Presidency during a term of office may be elected President to no more than one subsequent term. If the President anticipates or experiences a temporary inability to fulfill the duties of office, he or she shall publicly assign the presidential duties to the Vice President for the duration of the inability. If the President and Vice President both die in office, or suffer some other calamity such that their two offices are vacant at the same time, Congress shall speedily meet in joint session and appoint a new President for the remainder of the term of office. In that event, the new President within fourteen days shall appoint a new Vice President without the need for congressional approval. If not, Congress shall appoint a Vice President without delay. As salary, the President and Vice President shall receive four times the national average of gross ordinary income.

Section 3 The President shall be the commander-in-chief of all military forces of the United States. Congress shall have sole authority to declare a state of war or military conflict, upon agreement of two-thirds of Senators and two-thirds of Representatives. Congress shall also have sole authority to determine the rules of a war or military conflict, or declare a cessation of a state of war or military conflict, upon agreement of a majority of Senators and a majority of Representatives. Declarations of Congress, either to determine the rules, or cease states of war or military conflict, are not subject to veto by the President. The President shall have authority to immediately respond to protect national security in the event of a military attack upon the United States. Under all circumstances, the military forces of the United States are subject to the authority of the President, who in turn is subject to the authority of Congress. The President and federal executive authority shall receive foreign ambassadors and officials, and shall negotiate treaties and agreements with foreign powers, subject to ratification by two-thirds of Senators and two-thirds of Representatives.

Section 4 The President shall appoint Ambassadors, Justices of the Supreme Court and the High Court of Review, and federal executive branch department heads, if confirmed by a majority of Senators and a majority of Representatives. The President, Vice President and federal executive branch department heads shall fill lesser positions in their respective offices and departments at their discretion without the need for congressional approval. All executive branch appointees serve at the pleasure of the President. When Congress is in recess, the President may temporarily fill ambassadorial and department head vacancies within the executive branch as necessary until Congress considers and votes upon the appointments. Congress shall at all times provide funding and approve appointments sufficient for the smooth functioning of the federal executive.

Section 5 The President shall appear before each bi-monthly joint session of Congress, report on the state of the Union, and answer questions from members of Congress. The President has no power to convene or adjourn the Senate or House of Representatives, or Congress in joint session, nor to grant reprieves, commutations or pardons for criminal convictions, nor to immunize any person against criminal indictment or prosecution.

Article VI Federal Judiciary

The **Supreme Court**, and the **High Court of Review**, shall together direct the federal judicial authority, which shall be empowered and required to hear and decide all legal matters concerning the United States that are not internal to an individual State. The federal judiciary shall have sole authority to interpret this Re-Constitution and its amendments, and to ensure that the laws and actions of the government of the United States, and the individual States, do not violate this Re-Constitution or its amendments.

Section 1 The Supreme Court, and lower federal case courts under its direction that it creates as necessary, shall hear and decide all federal criminal and civil trials and appeals. The decisions of the Supreme Court and lower federal case courts shall be binding on all parties to the particular case, and constitutional interpretations expressed therein shall provide precedent for subsequent federal court cases. The decisions of the Supreme Court and lower federal case courts shall not become federal law, which shall be limited to this Re-Constitution, its amendments, and laws passed by Congress.

Section 2 The High Court of Review, and lower federal review courts under its direction that it creates as necessary, shall have authority to review and determine the constitutionality of all laws, and the lawfulness of all actions, of federal, state, and local government, except the judiciary, where deciding criminal and civil trials and appeals. The determination by the High Court or a lower federal review court that a law is unconstitutional, or a governmental action is unlawful, shall render that law or action null and void, and bars the government from enacting or enforcing the law, or committing the action. All legal complaints between different States, or between a State and the federal government, or between Congress and the federal executive branch, shall be heard and decided by the federal review courts.

Section 3 The Supreme Court and the High Court of Review shall each be comprised of nine **Justices**, appointed by the President as vacancies occur, and confirmed by a majority of Senators and a majority of Representatives. **Judges** of the lower federal case courts and review courts shall be appointed by their respective Justices, and confirmed by a majority of Senators and a majority of Representatives. All federal Justices and Judges shall serve without term until the age of eighty years on good behavior, subject to impeachment by Congress. Upon ratification of this Re-Constitution, all sitting Supreme Court Justices shall remain in office, unless they are eighty years or older. After the first general election following ratification of this Re-Constitution, the President, Senate and House of Representatives shall each appoint three High Court of Review Justices, to be confirmed by Congress, after which vacancies shall be filled by presidential appointment and congressional confirmation. As salary, Justices shall receive four times, and Judges three times, the national average of gross ordinary income. Congress shall at all times provide funding and approve appointments sufficient for the smooth functioning of the federal judiciary.

Article VII The States

Section 1 The **States** shall not through their laws or actions violate this Re-Constitution or its amendments, nor deny to any citizens of the United States their privileges, nor deny to any persons their civil liberties and rights as enumerated by this Re-Constitution and its amendments. Full faith and credit shall be given in each State to the laws and actions of every other State. Any person warranted for arrest in one State, found in another, shall be arrested in that State and delivered up to the warranting State. The States shall settle any disputes between themselves peaceably and in accordance with any federal adjudication thereof. Federal government shall not give preference to one State over another, nor mandate State actions for federal purposes without providing funding sufficient to accomplish the mandate. States shall provide a public education to their legal residents eighteen years of age or younger.

Section 2 No new States shall be added to the United States, nor shall any State secede from the United States. States shall not confederate between themselves or other corporate bodies, including foreign governments, nor lay charges for or otherwise restrict interstate commerce or transit. The boundaries between contiguous States are inviolable, and shall not be altered except by mutual agreement. The federal government shall secure the borders of the United States from illegal foreign entry, and protect the States from invasion or insurrection. Individual States shall have the authority to supplement federal measures to secure themselves from invasion, insurrection, or illegal foreign entry, as they deem necessary.

Article VIII Conduct of Elections

Section 1 **Elections for public office** within the United States, at all levels and branches of government, shall be conducted uniformly, with standards and practices to be established by Congress, so that voters and candidates enjoy the equal protection of uniform election laws and methodology throughout the United States. Electoral districts shall be drawn by non-partisan ad hoc citizens' commissions convened to create compact, competitive districts that avoid dividing locales and communities. All disputes concerning the conduct or results of elections shall be resolved at the level of government the disputed circumstances arose. No elective body shall be the judge of the results of any election for one of its positions. Incumbent public officials shall not use their office, or its resources, to campaign for or against candidates for public office.

Section 2 In all States and the District of Columbia general elections shall occur on the first Tuesday of November, primary elections on the first Tuesday of July, and special elections on the first Tuesday of March. Congressional terms of office shall begin and end on the second Monday of January. Presidential and Vice-Presidential terms of office shall begin and end on the third Monday of January. All citizens elected or appointed to public office shall swear or affirm loyalty to the United States and fiduciary obligation to its citizens before assuming office, and hold only one salaried position at any given time, during and after which they shall not enjoy immunity from liability for misdeeds committed while in office. No elected public official shall accept or fail to return campaign contributions from parties negotiating with, doing business for, or seeking permits or special benefits from any agency of government over which he or she has official influence. All public officials shall disclose any apparent, potential or actual conflicts of interest in fulfilling their public duties, and shall recuse themselves where the conflicts of interest cannot be eliminated. It shall be a criminal offense for citizens to accept or knowingly receive any gift, offering or compensation, or otherwise profit beyond their lawfully determined salary and benefits, as a consequence of their public office. No changes in salary or benefits for any public office shall be retroactive, nor apply to the persons legislating or authorizing the changes, during their tenure in office.

Section 3 Elections for public office within the United States, at all levels and branches of government, shall be conducted fairly, so that citizens have an equal opportunity to compete for public office on the basis of their talents and fitness to serve. Citizens seeking public office shall gather endorsement signatures from eligible voters as a prerequisite for candidacy. Eligible voters may endorse only one prospective candidate per office. For each public office, the ten citizens who gather the greatest numbers of valid endorsement signatures shall then together take an objectively-graded written entrance exam, devised by the legislative authority to test the knowledge and judgment of the prospective candidates relevant to the office sought. The five highest test scorers shall qualify as candidates for the primary election, and shall be required to regularly debate one another, and be tested and examined by the public, in a variety of subjects, formats, and venues. All candidates for public office shall fulfill their mandatory electoral activities at public expense. For every election, all news media operating within the electoral jurisdiction shall be required at their expense to regularly broadcast and disseminate records of the debates, tests, examinations of and statements from the candidates. All news media operating within the electoral jurisdiction shall also be required at their expense to fairly broadcast and disseminate persons' diverse expressions of support for or opposition to candidates for public office. The two highest vote-getters in the July primary election shall qualify for the November general election, and again shall be required to participate in a variety of debates, tests and examinations as the public and governing legislative authority deem appropriate.

Section 4 Citizens seeking the Presidency shall gather signatures of eligible voters from the State of their residence, as a prerequisite for candidacy. Citizens residing in the District of Columbia shall do likewise. Each State and the District of Columbia shall test the ten resident citizens who gather the greatest numbers of valid endorsement signatures, the five highest test scorers to compete in that State's or the District of Columbia's presidential primary. The States and the District of Columbia shall separately conduct presidential primary elections on the first Tuesday in July for the presidential candidates residing in their respective State or the District of Columbia. Winners of the primaries from each State and the District of Columbia shall then participate in presidential secondary elections on the first Tuesday in September, organized into the following five regions:

West

Alaska, Arizona, California, Idaho, Hawaii, Nevada, New Mexico, Oregon, Utah, Washington

Middle West

Colorado, Kansas, Montana, Minnesota, Nebraska, North Dakota, Oklahoma, South Dakota, Texas, Wyoming

Central

Arkansas, Illinois, Indiana, Iowa, Kentucky, Michigan, Missouri, Ohio, Tennessee, Wisconsin

Southeast

Alabama, District of Columbia, Florida, Georgia, Louisiana, Maryland, Mississippi, North Carolina, South Carolina, Virginia, West Virginia

Northeast

Connecticut, Delaware, Maine, Massachusetts, New Hampshire, New Jersey, New York, Pennsylvania, Rhode Island, Vermont

The five winners from the regional secondary elections shall compete for the Presidency in a national general election on the first Tuesday in November. The winner shall become the President, and the runner-up shall become the Vice President.

Section 5 In each of the primary, secondary and general presidential elections, voters may vote for up to three different candidates in rank-order preference. No ballot shall allow voters to vote more than once for the same candidate. A first-place preference vote shall be valued as three points; a second-place preference vote shall be valued as two points; and a third-place preference vote shall be valued as one point. In any presidential election, the winner shall be the candidate who receives the highest point total. In the general presidential election, the runner-up shall be the candidate who receives the second-highest point total.

Section 6 As uniform and fair elections are the central mechanism of representative democracy, Congress and State legislatures shall maintain stringent criminal penalties for violations of the conduct of elections as provisioned in this Re-Constitution and its amendments, and as elaborated by Congress and State legislatures.

Article IX Citizens' Power of Referendum

In order to directly check and balance federal legislative and executive authority, the citizens of the United States shall have the power of **Referendum**, to reverse and render null and void federal laws or actions, with the exception of judicial decisions, this Re-Constitution and its amendments. Referendums shall be initiated upon the authorization of a majority of State legislatures or State ballot initiatives. In that event a national plebiscite shall be scheduled by Congress for the first Tuesday in March, July, or November, whichever comes first. Once a referendum has been initiated, the federal law or action to be referended shall be held in abeyance, without effect, while it is challenged by referendum. The agreement of a majority of citizens voting in the referendum election shall reverse and render null and void the federal law or action in question.

Article X Citizens' Power of Ratification

If authorized by two-thirds of the States, Congress shall schedule a special national plebiscite for the citizens of the United States to vote upon **Ratification** of this Re-Constitution. Ratification shall be approved upon the agreement of a majority of citizens voting in the special election.

Article XI Citizens' Power of Amendment

If authorized by two-thirds of the States, Congress shall schedule a special national plebiscite for the citizens of the United States to vote upon any proposed **Amendments** to this Re-Constitution. States must authorize exactly the same language for any proposed amendment. Amendments shall be approved upon the agreement of a majority of citizens voting in the special election.

EXPLICATION OF THE PROPOSED RE-CONSTITUTION, WITH COMPARISONS TO OUR EXISTING CONSTITUTION

Proceeding from the Preamble through the Articles and Sections, there will be many references to the proposed Re-Constitution, and to our existing Constitution. For brevity's sake within the text to follow, they shall be abbreviated respectively ***Re-Con*** and ***Ex-Con***.

Preamble

The differences between the preambles begin immediately: rather than "We the People," Re-Con starts with "We the Citizens." The difference underscores a recurring problem with Ex-Con: it is imprecise as often as it is poetic, and the poetry can disguise an ugly truth. In this case, all the unenfranchised women, slaves, freedmen, Native Americans and white men without sufficient property or wealth may have rightly asked *which* people Ex-Con's preamble referred to by the words "We the People" written as a banner *ten times the height* of the rest of the text. As a matter of fact, Ex-Con was "ordained and established" by a select minority of the people. Re-Con instead refers to "We the Citizens" as those who would vote to replace Ex-Con.

Lists vs. Concepts

Preambles are a summary statement of the purpose of the document to follow. Ex-Con does so in a characteristic fashion, by providing a *list* of goals (more perfect Union, justice, domestic tranquility, common defense, general welfare, liberty). This is a recurring technique in Ex-Con, for example when *enumerating* (listing) powers of the federal government. The problem with lists is that they either leave things out, or unforeseeable new goals and needs arise. That is why Ex-Con's Article I Section 8 tacks on the 'necessary and proper' clause at its close: the preceding list of congressional powers may require some action or measure to bring the power into effect that they didn't (or couldn't) think of. Re-Con avoids listmaking, wherever possible employing a *conceptual* rather than enumerative description. The concept is designed to express a principle, that can then be used to interpret future unforeseeable constitutional issues.

Re-Con Goal #1: Democracy

Nevertheless Re-Con's preamble does specify goals. First, it introduces a word in its first sentence that does not appear anywhere in Ex-Con: *democracy*. The stated goal is to perfect our representative (i.e., indirect) democracy, which is defined by borrowing Lincoln's 'of, by and for' language from the Gettysburg address, on behalf of the citizens of our republic. This purpose is articulated first, to emphasize its primacy.

A Republic Becoming a Democracy

A note on terminology within the first stated goal: while democracy ('rule of the people') and republic ('thing of the public') have etymologies that sound alike, *republic* has been applied historically to a much wider range of governments, often contrasted with monarchy or tyranny, and in which the general public may have some limited or partial participation. We are a republic, in the process of perfecting a representative democracy.

Re-Con Goal #2: Expansion of Rights

Re-Con's second stated goal in its preamble is to expand our civil liberties and rights. Most of the rights we enjoy under Ex-Con were literally an afterthought, introduced as amendments after Ex-Con was ratified. We have been playing catchup ever since. Civil liberties and rights are treated early and comprehensively in Re-Con.

Re-Con Goal #3: Improve Our Federalism

The third and last stated goal in Re-Con's preamble is to improve our federalism, as a key to preserving and protecting the Union itself. The relationship between state and federal governments within our national framework is redefined by Re-Con in a variety of ways.

Article I: Citizenship

Re-Con addresses issues of citizenship in its first article, before all other subjects, as an attempt to underscore its centrality to the concept of a nation. A nation is a sovereign group of people – a body politic with a government – occupying and controlling a geographic portion of the planet. Its citizens are the members of that group. The first constitutional question is how one should achieve the status of a citizen, a member of a nation.

Ex-Con: Citizenship Conferred by Place of Birth

Our Ex-Con did not address this question until the Fourteenth Amendment, almost eighty years after Ex-Con was originally ratified. It was written, along with the Thirteenth and Fifteenth Amendments, to drive constitutional nails into the coffin of slavery. Its key provision as to citizenship is that anyone born in the United States is thereby a citizen. Since by that time virtually all ex-slaves were native-born, they automatically achieved citizenship. A phrase was attached – "and subject to the jurisdiction thereof" – that has been interpreted as applying to anyone not representing a foreign government.

As a consequence, if a woman enters the United States without permission, and has a child, that child is a citizen. If a woman lawfully visits the United States temporarily, for the purpose of giving birth on American soil, her child is a citizen. Even if a pregnant woman lawfully visits the United States, with the intention to return to her country of origin to give birth, but unexpectedly gives early birth on American soil, that child is a citizen.

Re-Con: Citizenship Through Naturalization or Parentage

Re-Con takes an entirely different approach to citizenship. It is not accorded a status that can be achieved as a result of an illegal act, or a lawful ploy, or a pure accident. Citizenship under Re-Con is treated somewhat like a type of personal property, a prized possession that is designed to be earned (through naturalization), owned and enjoyed and shared with one's offspring. It is not treated as a right, but a privilege, whose prerogatives can be circumscribed or revoked by due process of federal law upon conviction of (statutorily determined) high crimes. Under Re-Con, many of the adult privileges and obligations of a citizen (ability to vote, serve in public office, on juries, etc.) begin at the age of eighteen.

The reason Re-Con takes the polar opposite attitude toward citizenship than Ex-Con, is because the system we have does not sufficiently value citizenship. Our society should make being a member (citizen) of this club (nation) as big a deal as possible, in as many ways as possible, to treat it as the extraordinary privilege it indeed is.

Citizenship Privileges, Not Rights

It should be emphasized that a treatment of citizenship prerogatives as privileges, not rights, aligns with Re-Con's definition of a right/freedom as something that must apply equally to everyone, across the entire planet, whether or not a person is currently able to exercise and enjoy that right/freedom.

Under this definition, citizenship prerogatives are never treated by governments as rights. Of the two-hundred-plus nations around the world, none of them permits anyone who wishes to become a citizen, much less enter or leave the country with free, unquestioned, unexamined, undocumented transit. One can argue that we *should* have free transit and universal citizenship, and in the future, we just might. But today, nations consider that their sovereignty includes the power to dictate policy on such matters. Passports, visas, citizenship status, these are privileges that every government treats differently *and changes at will*.

It also should be acknowledged that any privilege that is not earned, but automatically granted, is likely less precious in the mind of the possessor than something that is earned. For that reason a naturalized citizen in many cases swells with greater pride than a natural-born citizen. It is something that he or she has *earned*. The child (and grandchild, etc.) of that naturalized citizen will on average swell with less pride, because they didn't earn it.

Article II: Branches and Levels of Government

Separation of powers is one of the key elements in Ex-Con, and it is designed to be preserved and strengthened through clarification in Re-Con. First, the purpose of separating powers, that each part of government check and balance the powers of every other part, is made explicit in Re-Con. Second, government is described like a nine-square tictactoe board: three levels down (federal, state, local) and three branches across (legislative, executive, judicial).

Enumerating Federal Powers Has Not Controlled Their Extent

If there was one overriding reason the Framers met in 1787, it was because the Articles of Confederation had created a loose quasi-federal structure that just wasn't working. Without a federal umbrella overarching the States with real authority, the confederation was threatening to blow apart into separate conflicting and possibly warring States.

Ex-Con solved this problem in an appropriately cautious manner, by listing the powers that the federal government would have over and between the States. As mentioned above, Ex-Con's Article I Section 8 added the necessary-and-proper clause in recognition that enumerated powers would require unenumerated measures to implement their provisions. The Tenth Amendment quickly reinforced the same principle of specific enumeration of federal powers, stating that any power *not* delegated to the federal government (or prohibited to the States) by Ex-Con was retained by the States or the people. Keeping federal powers closely defined and in check was clearly a priority from the outset.

Even so, it didn't take long before it became clear that some of the relations between the States that the federal government needed to have power over weren't specifically mentioned. To deal with this, certain Section 8 powers, such as the commerce clause ("To regulate commerce...among the several states..."), have been stretched in meaning when necessary to justify a federal power. While the elasticity of the necessary-and-proper and commerce clauses (among others) has showcased the creativity of our politicians, judges and justices over the decades, the exercise only underscores the inadequacy of an enumerative approach to government powers. Lists are never exhaustive, and new unforeseeable issues will forever arise.

A Conceptual Division of State/Federal Powers

To address this problem, Re-Con makes a conceptual division of powers between the levels and branches of government, without an attempt at enumeration. Concerning federal powers, "Federal authority and law shall extend to all matters between or shared by the States, all matters external to the United States, and the District of Columbia." Conversely, concerning State powers, "A State's authority and law shall extend to all matters internal to that State...."

Government's Proper Role in Commerce

Article II includes a clause – "Wherever reasonable alternatives exist, government shall not practice commerce" – whose purpose is to limit government engagement in commercial enterprise. When government practices commerce (offering goods or services for a price) in competition with private enterprise it does so unfairly, because government inevitably tilts the playing field to its advantage. Situations where government has the field to itself, practicing monopoly commerce, are equally undesirable: the absence of competition encourages laxity, incompetence and bloated pricing. The ideal Re-Con seeks to encourage is a government that both regulates and facilitates private business activity, while eschewing any commercial enterprise of its own, deferring commerce to the private (both for-profit and non-profit) sector wherever possible.

Examples where government needs to offer its own public-sector service or good for a price, because no private-sector alternative is feasible, include issuance of licenses (marriage, driver's, business, occupational, etc.), vehicle and other registrations, permits of various kinds, postal services, passports, visas, and so on. While one can easily imagine private businesses outperforming a typical department of motor vehicles, or delivery companies competing to offer postal services better, faster and cheaper, government should retain provision of public services whenever technical and security concerns dictate. With each service those concerns can of course change over time, rendering reasonable private-sector alternatives possible.

Examples where government should not conduct business, because reasonable private-sector alternatives already exist, are equally numerous. Public agencies have accumulated a wide variety of properties and businesses that often can and in many cases should be privately operated: vehicle inspection sites, hospitals, clinics, pharmacies, housing complexes, senior centers, athletic stadiums, exercise clubs, swimming pools, golf courses, ski resorts, marinas, recycling centers, even liquor stores and smoke shops, to name a few. In some cases, these publicly-owned properties and businesses can either be sold, or if public ownership is retained (as it often should be), to lease their management through competitive bidding to private enterprises specializing in that particular type of property or business. 'Enterprise' partnerships between public owners and private managers have become increasingly popular, and mostly successful. If the lessee is unsatisfactory, they can be removed and replaced with another. The end result is better service at a better price. And government confines itself to its proper role of governing commerce, not practicing it.

The above discussion should not be misinterpreted to encourage government to hand over management of public non-commercial institutions to private companies. Prisons come quickly to mind. They're not commercial enterprises, and should not be treated as such. For-profit prison corporations have perverse incentives to retain their inmates, and 'care' for them as cheaply as possible.

Supremacy and Transparency

Re-Con, like Ex-Con, has a supremacy clause, providing that the federal constitution, its amendments, and all federal laws and treaties in conformity with the constitution, have authority over all nine squares of the tictactoe board. Article II then closes with a transparency clause, requiring that all government proceedings be conducted publicly whenever possible (exceptions may include national security and intelligence matters, personal privacy protections, etc.), and that records of the public proceedings be freely and widely available.

Article III: Enumeration of Civil Liberties and Rights

Having made an argument against the effectiveness of enumerations when dividing State and federal powers, when it comes to civil liberties and rights, the opposite is true: fundamental rights should be listed, and in detail sufficient to ensure their protection. Before examining the list, some preliminary points need to be made.

Liberties, Freedoms, Rights

First, concerning terminology, three terms (liberties, freedoms, rights) are always floating around one another on this subject; their use will be simplified for the purposes of Re-Con. 'Liberty' and 'freedom' sound a lot alike, and most dictionaries will use freedom to define liberty, and liberty to define freedom. Their usage is slightly different, however. 'Liberty' often is used in a narrower sense, to refer to civil and political contexts ("Give me liberty, or give me death"). 'Freedom' is used more broadly. It also has an adjectival form, which makes it more versatile (free will, free association, free country, etc.). For our purposes, no substantive difference in meaning will be intended between liberty and freedom. If you have one, you have them both. Concerning 'rights,' it has already been argued that any right can be boiled down to a 'to' freedom (to do or not to do) and/or a 'from' freedom (immunity or protection from a detriment, such as harm, damage or loss).

Rights Apply Equally to All Persons

Second, to whom do the enumerated rights/freedoms apply in Re-Con? They apply equally to all persons (not only citizens) within all the States, the District of Columbia, and all territories and possessions of the U.S. The only exception is made for those "Persons apprehended making war against the United States, or assisting in the furtherance thereof...." Those persons are "subject to military law and justice." Because this important matter is referred to only once in the text, we will digress to examine at some length the unique circumstance where rights do not apply, before proceeding to explicate Re-Con's enumeration of civil rights and freedoms.

Arrest (Criminal) vs. Apprehension (Military)

There are three basic categories in which a government lawfully takes a person into custody. In the first category, a person may be arrested for an alleged crime, and all of the relevant criminal arrest and trial protections listed in Re-Con's Article III apply. In the second and third categories, a person is apprehended or captured while purportedly making war against the United States, or assisting in furthering the warmaking, to which Re-Con's protections do not apply. The distinction between the second and third categories lies in whether the apprehended person is considered a lawful combatant (an identifiable soldier, for example) or an unlawful combatant (examples are a spy, saboteur, or terrorist). Military law and justice treat these two categories very differently: in the former, a captured soldier is held as a prisoner of war for the duration of the conflict, and then released and returned to his or her country of origin; in the latter case, someone considered an unlawful combatant may be tried, not by a civil court, but by a military tribunal, under its own rules of procedure, standards of evidence and proof, and applicable punishments. An examination of rights pertaining to criminal arrest and trial in Re-Con's Article III Section 10 will demonstrate the many ways (Miranda rights, search warrants, etc.) they do not readily apply to apprehensions, detentions or trials of wartime combatants.

Enemy Combatants and Habeas Corpus

Our Supreme Court, in its post-9/11 decisions, has proceeded from the premise that enemy combatants have the right to a writ of habeas corpus (to challenge their detention in a federal court of law), if they're held anywhere on American soil. That premise is based on Ex-Con's Article I Section 9, which states that the writ can only be suspended if public safety is endangered in the event of rebellion or invasion. Since rebellion or invasion can by definition only occur *within* the country, it follows that – barring conditions of rebellion or invasion – everyone who is held in detention within the United States has a right to a habeas corpus hearing in court. Some lines of legal reasoning have accorded a clearer right to American citizens, but Ex-Con doesn't make any citizenship distinctions in regard to habeas corpus, so everyone means everyone.

That's why the military has favored Cuba's Guantanamo Bay, which the U.S. occupies under renewable leases, as the place of choice to hold high-value enemy combatants: it's not American soil, yet nearby, easy to supply and defend, and a long ways from the Middle East. The Supreme Court upended that strategy by determining that although Guantanamo is indeed on foreign soil, our military controls the district, so it is a de facto American possession and thus falls within the jurisdiction of federal courts. This spurred our military and intelligence agencies to increase their ongoing practice of rendition – secretly transporting captives to the darkest corners of the globe for interrogation beyond the reach of legal authority – because now detainees at Guantanamo, and perhaps other overseas American installations, could not only exercise their right of habeas corpus, they could describe in open court the conditions under which they were being held.

Rendition soon acquired yet another rationale, because enemy combatants held in Guantanamo who challenged their detentions in federal court found they had a good chance of success. Once they were in civil court, the strictures of civil due process came into play. The military was forced to defend its detentions with one hand tied behind its back: it couldn't present evidence that would reveal its tactics or sources; witnesses – who at any rate couldn't easily return from theaters of war – might put themselves or their operations at risk if their identities were revealed in open court; and of course procedures normally required in criminal arrest had not been followed. In response, federal courts tinkered with habeas corpus due process to favor the government, giving it a rebuttable presumption in favor of the detention, or looser testimonial and material evidentiary standards. In other words, to improve the government's odds in habeas corpus hearings, federal courts improvised sawed-off versions of due process for the combatants. But a half-way house of rights for anyone, even an enemy combatant, is a rabbit hole we can't go down. There has to be a more legally coherent way to provide combatants a real opportunity to challenge their detention, without the courts hobbling them with a residue of due-process rights.

Judicial Review of Military Detentions

Our post-9/11 enemy combatant jurisprudence went off the rails right out of the station, when it wrongly assumed that belligerents in war have any civil rights after capture. Re-Con instead cleaves to the long-held (harsh but accurate) understanding that those apprehended while warmaking are not owed the protection of any civil rights by their capturers. Any privileges prisoners receive are in fact grants, acts of mercy. The first act of mercy is taking them prisoner, rather than killing them, as customarily occurred until very recent history. Other conditions of confinement, like those agreed to in the Geneva Conventions, are a product of enlightened self-interest: one country treats its prisoners humanely, in the hope that other warring countries will reciprocate and do the same.

Under Re-Con all civil rights are intended to apply equally to everyone, irrespective of whether the persons are American citizens. Conversely, the absence of civil rights for apprehended wartime belligerents is also equally applied irrespective of citizenship. Just as we do not consider citizenship status with respect to the equal protection of our rights, neither should we distinguish citizens from non-citizens when considering the disposition of wartime detainees. Citizens making war against their own country, if captured, have not earned preferential treatment over that accorded foreign belligerents. Some might argue they deserve worse. Re-Con would accord captured belligerents – citizens or foreign – equal treatment.

The critical problem Re-Con attempts to address is that mistaken captures – especially in the fog of war – are inevitable: persons are sometimes wrongly apprehended as warmakers when in fact they are not. Our military uses battlefield 'identity' hearings to weed out non-combatants wrongly apprehended. That is a useful frontline filter, but persons must also have an avenue to challenge their detention outside of military authority. Re-Con provides that avenue through newly-created federal review courts (see Article VI discussion below). What standards would the review courts use to judge a detention's legitimacy?

This is where Congress must play its role. Under Re-Con, as under Ex-Con, it is Congress that declares war. Because every war is different, Congress must also define the rules by which that war is to be conducted. For example, the 'war on terror' has been waged mainly against non-state actors, who conduct their warmaking much differently than a state actor. In this new type of war, the Geneva Conventions haven't been much help, as they only address wars between nations. Article V of the Third Geneva Convention calls for a "competent tribunal" to distinguish lawful from unlawful combatants, which Congress can create through military tribunals and commissions.

When it declares war, Congress needs to describe the standards by which federal review courts shall evaluate detentions – and military tribunals – during that particular conflict. Those same standards become the rules of conduct the military (and commander-in-chief) are directed to follow in their prosecution of the war. If Congress declares war, or authorizes the use of military force, but does *not* also sufficiently dictate rules for that conflict, neither the military, nor the federal review courts overseeing it, are given the direction they need to properly fulfill their roles. Under our system that has often proven to be an unfortunate likelihood. No doubt there are practical, historical reasons why Congress is reluctant to embrace its role in defining the rules of war, instead taking a back seat to the military. Thankfully, a large part of the remedy can be constitutional.

Declarations of War

Ex-Con's Article I Section 8 provisions concerning declarations of war are structurally inadequate to guarantee Congress's control over the process. The terse language ("The Congress shall have the power...to declare war...and make rules concerning captures on land and water....") would appear to do the job. It implies that a simple majority of both houses is sufficient for a declaration of war. The President can veto the declaration, which a two-thirds supermajority can then override. A vote of Congress to conclude a war would follow a parallel procedure.

Two defects form bookends to Ex-Con's process. On the front end, so long as the President agrees, a simple majority can start a war. If there is any issue that cries out for greater consensus, it is the momentous decision to go to war. A narrow majority should not decide the matter. And if

Congress acts despite significant opposition, or in haste, they are unlikely to adequately spell out the rules of the conflict. If Congress later decides during the conflict to pass follow-up legislation regulating the conduct of the war, the horse may already be out of the barn; a President can accuse the legislators of second-guessing the military in an ongoing conflict, and veto the measure. In that instance Congress, to impose its will, must climb a steep, two-thirds acclivity in a storm of reaction. It is more likely the war will continue without the needed rules.

On the back end, if Congress votes to end a war, but the President disagrees, without a two-thirds override the war goes on. In that case, if any more than half the members of Congress no longer wish to continue, it is safe to assume that a comparable percentage of the public (and military) has a similar opinion. Yet a President who wants to press on can hold an unwilling majority hostage to his or her wishes, unless defied by at least two out of three congresspersons.

Re-Con takes the President out of the equation, leaving political decisions about war entirely to Congress. A declaration of war would in all cases require a two-thirds supermajority, to ensure that a solid consensus supports the cause, and that a narrow partisan majority has not become enraptured by a momentary intemperance. Declarations of the rules of conduct, or of a cessation of war, would have a lower threshold: a simple majority of Congress. In any event, the decisions Congress makes to start a war, to determine the rules of its conduct, and to end the war, would not be subject to presidential veto.

Re-Con includes a complementary provision: executive orders on any subject can be nullified by an act of Congress, again without the possibility of a presidential veto. Under Ex-Con a President can issue any executive order, wait almost two weeks before vetoing an act of Congress attempting to reverse it, then wage a political fight against a two-thirds override, all the while carrying out whatever actions he or she pleases for a period spanning weeks. Ex-Con grants far too much unilateral power for a President to safely possess in a democracy. In contrast, Re-Con provides a one-step reversal for the errant executive order: a simple majority vote of Congress.

Treason

Ex-Con's Article III Section 3 states that "Treason against the United States shall consist only in levying war against them, or in adhering to their enemies, giving them aid and comfort." 'Enemies' has been narrowly interpreted to mean only those actually waging war against us: mere adversaries don't count. And although a literal reading of Ex-Con would imply that anyone can commit treason, our statutory law states that it only applies to those "owing allegiance" to the United States, primarily citizens or those who have applied to be citizens. So under Ex-Con, in order for a person to commit treason, the country must first be at war, and the traitor must be a citizen (or wannabe citizen) working for the other side.

The reader can see that we're running up against the same problem with traitors that we did with enemy combatants. While their apprehension will necessarily occur during wartime, Ex-Con defines treason as a crime (the only crime defined in Ex-Con). Therefore an accused traitor will be tried in civil court either with all the protections accorded any other criminal defendant, or a sawed-off version of due process akin to that applied to enemy combatants. In any case the extraordinary circumstances attending the wartime actions, pursuit, capture, detention and prosecution of a traitor will not fit the civil procedural mold. No wonder there have been very few treason trials in American history, and even fewer convictions.

Re-Con makes no mention of treason in its text. Instead, Re-Con states that "Persons apprehended making war against the United States, or assisting in the furtherance thereof, shall be subject to military law and justice," language intended to include both enemy combatants *and* (what are otherwise referred to as) traitors. The two categories would have equal access to the federal review courts to challenge their detentions, but without any 'rights' beyond the rules Congress has established for the war during which they were apprehended. Re-Con's folding of treason into the larger class of combatancy is not intended to preclude statutory law against forms of criminal disloyalty. Nor is it intended to deprive anyone the pleasure of continuing to use 'traitor' and 'treason' as all-purpose political swearwords.

Explication of Enumerated Rights/Freedoms

Each right/freedom listed in Article III will not be treated in detail. The reader will note that while the particular rights subject may appear boilerplate, it is given exact, detailed language intended to delineate the application of the right, and to eliminate any wiggle room for government to violate it. The only rights that will be elucidated here are those that do not appear in Ex-Con, or that Re-Con treats quite differently.

Discrimination

Ex-Con was written at a time when discrimination – in broad terms, the prejudicial mistreatment of persons – was widely practiced and accepted in society. The worst form of discrimination, slavery, was permitted under Ex-Con, where slaves are obliquely referred to as persons "held to service or labor." The Bill of Rights and later amendments prohibit a small number of specific forms of discrimination (most importantly the Thirteenth Amendment abolishing slavery).

Some of the few protections provided by Ex-Con's amendments dim under inspection. For example, Ex-Con's First Amendment prohibits Congress from establishing a federal religion or restricting religious exercise. Sounds good, but at that time different States favored (or disfavored) different Christian denominations, not to mention non-Christian religions. The First Amendment was designed to assure the States that Congress would practice neutrality on the issue, not putting its thumb on the scale for or against State-favored denominations; this assurance added heft to Ex-Con's Article VI guarantee that no religious test could ever be required for federal office. Nevertheless, the States remained free to continue practicing all the religious preference and discrimination they wanted.

The Fifth Amendment guarantees all persons due process under federal law. Yet a mere fourteen months after the Bill of Rights' passage, Congress passed a fugitive slave act that shredded due process, permitting a presumed runaway to be seized by a purported owner or agent anywhere in the States or territories. The claimant could then testify or present an affidavit to any local court. The process was so slipshod and biased in favor of the claimant, thousands of freedmen were wrongly identified as runaway slaves and returned to bondage.

The post-Civil War amendments attempted to take quantum leaps forward against discrimination. Not only was slavery outlawed, native-born ex-slaves were granted citizenship, and all citizens the right to vote (if they were men). The Fourteenth Amendment prohibited States from denying anyone due process, or the equal protection of their laws. Again, sounds good.

But as we all know, States observed these new strictures in the breach. African-Americans did not come to enjoy due process, or equal protection, or the unfettered right to vote. Native Americans were decimated by genocide. Asian and other immigrants suffered blatantly prejudicial mistreatment, even outright exclusions. All the while our judiciary repeatedly endorsed a dizzying panoply of discriminatory practices. Later amendments, granting women the franchise and outlawing poll taxes, did make crucial advances.

Discrimination however continues to be practiced in myriad ways that simply are not addressed in Ex-Con. As a result, in the absence of an overarching constitutional prohibition, many of our protections against prejudicial mistreatment – such as they are – rely for the most part on relatively recent federal and (varying) State statutory law. We need systemic protections against discrimination in housing, credit, employment, education, criminal and civil justice, voting, access to public and private amenities, and more. Given the pervasiveness of the problem, it appears we will never have enough statutory fingers to fill all the discriminatory holes that keep perforating our dike. Our piecemeal, whack-a-mole approach is not working.

Re-Con advocates a systematic frontal assault on prejudicial mistreatment through an explicit constitutional guarantee of freedom from discrimination. No less than a dozen parameters of prejudice are proscribed (we may need more). The importance of the subject is underscored by its appearance as the second listed civil liberty, preceded only by freedom from slavery and involuntary servitude.

Two characteristics of discrimination should be contemplated. First, that our aversion to prejudicial mistreatment is a relatively modern instinct, roughly concomitant with our growing attraction to democracy. That makes sense, because democracy's ideal is for everyone to enjoy equal political rights, i.e., no discrimination in voting or running for office. The same instinct, broadened to a wider lens, encompasses a desire that all persons enjoy the same opportunities and access to the full spectrum of society's benefits and offerings. Democracy at its core is anti-discriminatory.

Second, in order to defeat discrimination, we must acknowledge that it is extremely deep-seated, even primal. Consider yourself one of the earliest humans, newly arrived on the savannah, struggling to survive against predators, human and animal. You can go it alone, but as a loner you are outnumbered: how will you ever prevail against other animals and humans who have coalesced into groups? So you quite naturally form alliances of mutual protection with other humans. Safety exists in numbers, as we say, but numbers also mean dominance.

The group you belong to will quickly develop an identity based on shared interests and characteristics. Anyone outside of your group will be recognized by perceived or actual differences. The differences can assume any form, as they do today. It can be skin color, lineage, language, territorial origin, social and cultural practices, religion, etc. You will naturally identify anyone not sharing your group's characteristics as 'others,' dangerous to your survival and unwelcome. You will either avoid or attempt to overwhelm those perceived as outsiders.

Over the eons the perceived or actual differences of other groups inevitably become imbedded as deep societal prejudices, invoking fear, hatred, bigotry, and a seemingly justified discrimination of others. So long as humans struggle and compete with one another to survive and flourish, they will continue to coalesce into groups of common interest that self-identify by their perceived or actual differences from outsiders. Primal habits die hard. At this stage our best step forward is to have a blanket constitutional protection against discrimination, while cultivating a society-wide appreciation for the benefits of cooperation and tolerance.

Eminent Domain

The last twelve words of Ex-Con's Fifth Amendment ("...nor shall private property be taken for public use, without just compensation") are succinct, yet the Supreme Court has repeatedly twisted their meaning beyond recognition. The justices have long clung to the ruse that somehow 'public use' should be construed to include 'public purpose,' a phrase that can be stretched to mean anything. This concoction has green-lighted government to take private property from one owner, and give or sell it to another (preferred) private owner for a purported 'public purpose.' In practice, it has invited political favoritism, seizing a coveted property from a hapless owner and conveying it to a recipient owner with clout and connections.

Re-Con's Article III Section 7 eliminates the possibility of such eminent domain abuses with an explicit statement that any private property taken by the government "shall be owned by the public for its use." It further provides that the owner be "compensated at fair market value for the property taken," and that if the government offers the seized property for sale at a future date, "The original owner or designated heir(s) shall have first right of refusal to purchase the property at fair market value...."

Homelessness

Within Article III, the first wholly new idea is Section 8, where homelessness is addressed from a public health and safety perspective. On the one hand, Re-Con requires government to provide sufficient housing for all persons without a home. This responsibility would inevitably devolve onto local municipal and county government, with assistance from State and federal authority to include food, clothing, medical care, counseling, and job training as necessary. On the other hand, vagrancy is prohibited: no one may live outside. Everyone has a home provided for them, whether they want it or not.

At first glance, this provision may appear draconian, or at the very least, not suitable for constitutional treatment. The argument in favor of an unwavering constitutional policy is our abject failure to solve the problem. After decades of policy experiments and mountains of largely wasted money, the situation is worse than ever. It is nothing less than a national disgrace. And the only Re-Con imposition on the indigent is that they cannot sleep outside.

Privacy Rights

Re-Con's Article III Section 9 significantly expands privacy protections, a subject that is treated by Ex-Con chiefly in its Fourth Amendment context of searches and seizures. Re-Con's Clause A is intended to be a tightening on that aspect of privacy.

Whereas Ex-Con lists "persons, houses, papers, and effects" as secure against "unreasonable searches and seizures," Re-Con instead employs more comprehensive language: "To be secure upon private property against searches and seizures without written warrant...." Ex-Con's expansive modifier *unreasonable* is omitted in Re-Con because it has invited judicial endorsement of non-warranted searches and seizures.

Private property is used in Re-Con instead of Ex-Con's list of "persons, houses, papers, and effects" because Ex-Con doesn't mention real (i.e., non-personal) property other than a house. The Supreme Court has interpreted that omission to allow non-warranted searches and seizures on private property apart from the house and its 'curtilage' (immediate surrounding area). As a result, under Ex-Con it is considered entirely legal for government to enter a private property's 'open fields' (beyond the house's curtilage) without the owner's knowledge or permission to conduct warrantless searches and seizures. 'Open fields' doctrine has even smiled upon surreptitiously setting up cameras for ongoing warrantless covert surveillance on private property. Re-Con's search-and-seizure language is crafted to prohibit these abuses.

Section 9 Clause B deals with an entirely different, and in some ways thoroughly modern, privacy realm. For lack of a more formal term, let's call it snooping.

Government, businesses and organizations, sometimes in concert, are going to great efforts to learn everything they can about us. Concerning the government, the privacy principle articulated is that whatever a member of the public cannot lawfully learn about us without our permission, the government should not be able to learn about us without first getting a warrant.

Concerning businesses and organizations, they learn many things about us in the course of our interactions with them, especially during our usage of their services or equipment. Under current law they are free to sell the personal data they have 'mined,' typically to advertisers who can then target the public with ever-greater precision.

Re-Con prohibits businesses or organizations from sharing any personal information with other businesses, organizations or individuals without our express permission and knowledge. Their request for permission must specify the information they wish to share, and with whom, and the reasons why. They are further prohibited from divulging anyone's personal information to the government without a warrant.

Protections for the Accused

Article III Section 10 details protections for the accused, in the event of arrest and trial, and departs from current practice in a variety of ways.

Section 10 Clauses B and C make a number of changes to pre-trial procedures:

• Clause B prohibits the public display or presentation of the accused in prison garb or restraints. This is a patently prejudicial practice, especially in the courtroom.

• Clause B also abolishes criminal grand juries. Ex-Con's Fifth Amendment requires "No person shall be held to answer for a capital, or otherwise infamous crime, unless on a presentment or indictment of a Grand Jury...." Without a definition of what an "otherwise infamous crime" might be, the practice has been to use grand juries to seek indictments for alleged federal felonies. States also have criminal grand juries, but only about half use them. In fact, across the globe, apparently only one other country still uses grand juries: Liberia, which borrowed Ex-Con's Fifth Amendment language for its nineteenth century constitution.

The reason criminal grand juries have been so widely abandoned is because they are prone to abuse. Prosecutors are allowed to examine individuals under subpoena without elementary procedural protections, including the presence of a judge or legal counsel, ability to give direct testimony, introduce exculpatory evidence, raise objections, or to question the mention or examine the presentation of purported evidence. The proceedings are conducted in secret and transcripts are sealed. Only a bare majority of jurors is required to return an indictment. Criminal grand juries are a dog and pony show for prosecutors, who not surprisingly procure indictments in the vast majority of cases. Grand juries began in English history as a way for a sovereign or central authority to elicit the assistance of local lords and gentry in support of an indictment and arrest. The centuries have not improved the process.

- Clause B prohibits detentions, either to question a suspect or witness, or to prevent the potential commission of a crime. One is either under arrest, or free to leave police custody.

- Clause C prohibits bail, because from the moment of arraignment, it discriminates against any accused person who happens to be of lesser means. This issue broaches a fundamental contradiction within our judicial system, particularly criminal proceedings: someone with less money receives less 'justice.' We have become so inured to this reality, that the absurdity of the fact doesn't elicit our opprobrium. The text below will attempt to adumbrate and correct the ways in which those accused of crime receive on average about as much 'justice' as they can afford. We will never have "one nation...with liberty and justice for all" unless we devise a judicial system where wealth (or its absence) and outcomes in court are decoupled and unrelated.

Section 10 Clause D requires that prosecution charges be specific and self-consistent. At present, prosecutors are often permitted to offer a menu of crimes, from which a jury may choose a 'lesser included charge,' if they are not convinced of the strongest charge. The problem with the menu of crimes is that they are often mutually exclusive of one another, requiring that a different set of facts be demonstrated beyond a reasonable doubt. For example, in a murder trial, the prosecutor may argue a first-degree (malice aforethought) crime, hoping the jurors will choose a 'lesser included' second-degree (intentional act, but unplanned, perhaps provoked, e.g., heat of passion) or voluntary manslaughter (intending harm but not death) conviction if not convinced of the first-degree charge. Choosing a different set of facts than the prosecutor presents in order to return a guilty verdict is not the proper function of a jury. A jury should decide whether the facts *as presented by the prosecutor* are true beyond a reasonable doubt. They should not be free to choose another, contradictory, set of facts in order to arrive at a guilty verdict.

Clause E of Section 10 prohibits testimony in criminal or civil trials from witnesses "who have received or been promised benefit in return for their testimony." The idea here is that all witness testimony should be impartial, and not subject to influence (or the appearance of influence) from benefit offered by one side or the other in a trial. Testimony in return for benefit from any partisan is inherently untrustworthy.

This prohibition is intended to exclude plea bargains as well as expert witnesses hired by either side in a case. If any principal in a trial wishes the court to hear expert testimony on any aspect of the proceedings, under Re-Con they are to make a request of the judge, who "shall subpoena impartial expert witnesses to testify without being informed who requested the expert opinions." A provision is attached that the experts shall be compensated at a rate sufficient to encourage their service.

Concerning plea bargains, it may be objected that prosecutors will no longer be able to leverage the 'little fish' to turn on the 'big fish' in a criminal enterprise. The little fish can still plead guilty and testify against their superiors under Re-Con. They would not however be acting on the promise of leniency for their cooperation; rather, they would be hoping through their testimony to elicit the mercy of the court during sentencing, something the grateful prosecutor could only recommend. In other words, negotiated 'deals' would no longer be permitted: little fish would take their chances with the court when they 'turn state's evidence.'

Section 10 Clause G is Re-Con's double jeopardy clause, and it is phrased to avoid any current abuses. For example, a person who is acquitted of murder in a criminal trial should be immunized from any 'wrongful death' civil suit which re-litigates the same factual territory.

Public Financing of Trial Costs

Section 12 of Article III is the second instance (after bail prohibition) in Re-Con where an attempt is made to eliminate a person's financial wherewithal as a factor in receiving justice through our courts. Under Ex-Con's Sixth Amendment, a person is guaranteed the opportunity for legal representation in the event of criminal arrest and trial. In practice, a person of greater means will hire a lawyer of their own choosing; a person of lesser means will be assigned a public defender. Under Re-Con, a person of any means may hire any lawyer to represent them, whether they are criminally charged or involved in a civil suit, and the lawyer will be publicly compensated at a rate sufficient to deter them from avoiding their public duty.

There are some catches here. If a person hires a lawyer to commence a civil action, but the court does not find the case triable, that person is responsible for the lawyer's expenses. Further, if a person loses at civil trial (unless against a public agency), he or she is responsible for the legal expenses of both sides. Finally, Section 12 concludes with a sentence prohibiting all forms of forfeiture, unless it is directed by a judicial judgment beyond appeal.

Restoring Rights of Contract

Ex-Con's Article I Section 10 prohibits States from passing laws "impairing the obligation of contracts." Ex-Con does not similarly enjoin the federal government; on the contrary, Ex-Con (Article I Section 8) gives Congress the power to make uniform federal bankruptcy laws, assumably with the possibility of debt relief, i.e., a modification of a debtor's obligations within a contract.

The plain language of the State prohibition was openly observed if quietly evaded by the courts until the 1930s, when a Minnesota law providing foreclosure relief in the depths of the Great Depression was upheld by the Supreme Court. Sympathy for the suffering public elicited a pragmatic massaging of the contract clause that was both understandable and regrettable. The camel's nose was now in the tent, and predictably, subsequent court decisions have found more rationales for State government to impair the obligation of contracts.

Re-Con's Article III Section 13 attempts to re-establish the durability of contract with the following categorical language: "Government shall not abrogate, nullify, or modify a legal, written contract between consenting parties." Unlike Ex-Con, no distinction is made between State and federal government in this regard. Nor is there a distinction between branches of government, which implies that courts can no longer set aside contractual obligations, as for example in bankruptcies. This judicial ability in bankruptcy court has led to abuses so rank, that periodically declaring bankruptcy has proven for some to be an effective business strategy. Under Re-Con, the most involvement government can have with respect to insolvency is to adjudicate or mediate between the contracting parties, or in special cases affecting a public interest, to fulfill on a party's behalf its contractual obligations.

Section 13 ends with language that should go without saying: government shall not "require persons to enter into contracts." A prerequisite of a valid contract is that the parties enter into it voluntarily, without compulsion or coercion. Requiring someone to enter into a contract renders it invalid.

Why prohibit the government from doing something that is so self-evidently unlawful?

Because that is precisely what the federal government did in the 'individual mandate' provision of the 2010 Affordable Care Act. Citing practical needs – to compel younger adults to buy health insurance, in order to offset the costs of caring for older adults; or to compel the uninsured to buy health insurance, so as not to shunt their costs onto the insured – the Act made it a violation of law for anyone not to have health insurance. But in order to have health insurance, an individual must enter into a contract with a health insurer. It is no less compelled if there are different policies or insurers to choose from. And it wasn't like auto or business insurance: you don't have to drive a car or own a business. But if you do, you need insurance, which makes a requirement of that kind lawful. You can opt out.

The individual mandate (since repealed federally) was different: it required *everyone* to be covered by a contract. All you had to do was be alive, and the insurance contract was mandatory. So if the government thought it was lawful to require that type of contract of us, just for being alive, perhaps there are others in the offing (life insurance?). Sad to say, the only surefire way to stop this overreach is with an explicit constitutional prohibition.

Executive and Legislative Use of Judicial Prerogatives

Re-Con's Article III Section 14 establishes that only a court of law can subpoena witnesses, or require an oath or affirmation of truthfulness, or punish any failure to appear or speak truthfully. At present, Congress also has these powers. This is a carryover from the English Parliament, which at the time Ex-Con was written very much intermingled legislative with judicial powers. For that reason, Ex-Con prohibits bills of attainder (where a legislature can find someone guilty of a high crime and effect punishment). Yet Ex-Con did not thoroughly cleanse our federal legislature of judicial prerogatives. One can ask, if Congress as a legislative body can subpoena witnesses, question them under oath and punish them if they refuse to answer or are believed to be untruthful, why can't state or even local legislative bodies not also have these powers? It would of course be a nightmare scenario for any city or county council, or state legislature, to have such prerogatives, but they are not a different political species from Congress. There is nothing in Ex-Con that stops them from exercising such powers.

Section 14 also addresses a similar issue with law enforcement or executive agencies, which at present can detain a person for questioning, and criminally prosecute that person for a supposed lack of truthfulness. Under Re-Con a person may lie to law enforcement, as indeed law enforcement can lie to a person, without fear of prosecution. This holds equally for legislative bodies: a person should not be required to appear, or swear an oath of truthfulness, or suffer reprisal for lying to Congress, as congresspersons are not punished for lying to the public. This creates an even playing field between the public on the one hand, and legislatures, law enforcement and executive agencies on the other hand: failure to appear, or refusing to answer questions or divulge information, or outright lying, should not ever be crimes unless under judicial oath or affirmation in a court of law.

Compensation for the Falsely Accused or Convicted

Section 15 of Article III requires that anyone who is damaged by a criminal investigation that does not result in charges, or charges that do not result in a conviction, or convictions that are subsequently overturned, be publicly compensated for their damages or losses. We are all familiar with stories of innocent persons who have suffered harm or whose homes have been damaged or destroyed by police searches or invasions, of criminal defendants who have been bankrupted while proving their innocence against unfounded charges, or of convicts who have lost years of their lives before being exonerated, who are never compensated for the damages they wrongly suffer.

A systemic failure to require compensation has two inevitable side effects: law enforcement is emboldened by this impunity to abuse its powers; and the public, well aware their lives can be destroyed regardless of their guilt, are intimidated from asserting their rights, especially to criticize government.

Unenumerated Rights

Re-Con does not have an equivalent to Ex-Con's Ninth Amendment, which states that Ex-Con's enumeration "of certain rights shall not be construed to deny or disparage others retained by the people." While the Ninth Amendment evinces a commendable caution in stating that rights other than those listed in Ex-Con do in fact exist, this constitutional point actually goes without saying. As discussed above in Pre-Constitution, in our society we share a numberless abundance of assumptions as to what elements our shared arenas of autonomy contain. Some implicit assumptions pertain to crucial rights, such as a person not being required to marry. Many are so obvious, and seemingly trivial (unless violated), we rarely even think about them. We consider ourselves free to choose how we groom ourselves, or what clothing we wear, or what we order in a restaurant, or what car we drive, and on and on and on. Re-Con's Article III lists the fundamental rights/freedoms that form the superstructure of a free society. But there are many other rights/freedoms we collectively take for granted, far too numerous to list.

'Substantive Due Process'

Although the Ninth Amendment would appear to be the logical place for American jurists to find justification for defending a right not enumerated in Ex-Con, that has not been the path more followed. Instead, a concept of 'substantive due process' has been introduced (to be distinguished from 'procedural due process') as latent within the shared language of the Fifth and Fourteenth Amendment due process clauses (persons shall not be deprived "of life, liberty, or property without due process of law").

A notion resembling due process got its start in our legal tradition with the Magna Carta, although the words 'due process' don't first appear in English law until more than a century later. The concept was clear enough: a person cannot be thrown in a dungeon, or have property confiscated, or be put to death, or whatever, unless a process of law is first followed, a process every person is due, i.e., owed.

A process is merely a series of connected actions, and in this context, a series of connected actions involving a case at law. Legal language normally distinguishes between a process or procedure in law, and the substance of a law, but there is inevitably a connection. If a person is denied a procedure in law (say, their day in court), they are obviously denied the substance of the law (say, protection of a fundamental right). But the distinction has a validity, in that it makes proper procedure in court a necessary condition of the proper application of the substance of a law. That is why a large matter of substance (a judgment or verdict) can be undone by a small failure of process: it's not too small, if it affects determination of the larger issue.

'Substantive due process' obfuscates the distinction between legal process and substance. The conflation becomes most evident when its contrasting phrase, 'procedural due process,' is analyzed. The words 'procedural' and 'process' derive from the same Latin verb ('to go forth'), and share meaning. 'Procedural due process' is from the Department of Redundancy Department, and 'substantive due process' sounds like an oxymoron. The courts don't need to employ a confusing legal phrase to identify an unenumerated right/freedom: there are a million of them, and if society disagrees with jurists over their finding and identification of an unenumerated right/freedom, we can pass a law declaring so.

Article IV: Federal Legislature

The basic bicameral structure of Congress is preserved in Re-Con, but a number of changes are proposed in order to reinvigorate a sagging institution.

Uniform Requirements and Terms of Congressional Office

The House and Senate are made more uniform in a number of details. They would have the same eligibility requirements: minimum age (twenty-five), citizenship (seven years), and residency (one year). They would also share the same four-year length of term. Under Ex-Con, the brief two-year stint in the House means the Representatives never stop campaigning for office, reducing their productivity, while the six-year Senate term is longer than virtually any other term of office for State or local legislators. Ex-Con prescribed such an extraordinary length of term in the Senate – triple that of the House – as a safeguard against democracy. As another cushion against the perceived whims of the people, the Framers assigned elections of Senators not to the general public, but to their respective State legislatures.

Congressional Term Limits

Representatives and Senators are subject to the same term limits under Re-Con. They may serve for no more than two consecutive four-year terms, but after sitting out a term, may run again for the same chamber. Term limits are necessary because the many advantages of incumbency result in *unfair* elections, with the same people occupying congressional seats for decades, sometimes for the remainder of their lives. The result is enfeebling: an out-of-touch gerontocracy – especially in the Senate – that can rival a Soviet politburo in age and ineffectiveness.

Fairness Doctrine

Fairness can be an elusive concept in everyday speech; in Re-Con it shall be defined as *equal opportunity*. Fairness doctrine arises in a variety of contexts in Re-Con. Earlier, it was applied to criminal arrest and prosecution, as well as civil litigation. In those contexts, it is undeniable that someone with more money will on average enjoy better treatment and results in the judicial system than someone with less money. That is unfair because two persons, merely because of a difference in their financial means, can be predicted to experience an unequal opportunity for justice. And as all reasonable people know in their guts, that in itself is unjust.

In an electoral context, as in the present discussion of congressional office, Re-Con applies a fairness doctrine to the unequal opportunity a challenger faces when attempting to unseat an incumbent. It is evident that incumbents at all levels of government are re-elected a far greater percentage of the time than their performance in office would appear to justify. The surefire way to solve that problem is to have term limits, with a proviso that after sitting out one term, the clock can start again.

Further along in Re-Con (see Article VIII discussion below), fairness doctrine is applied in an attempt to solve a related and even more serious electoral issue, the unequal opportunity presented by the greater or lesser amounts of money that candidates are able to spend on their campaigns for public office. Under our current system, all other factors being equal, the candidate with the biggest war chest has a better chance of winning. Re-Con offers a solution to this seemingly intractable problem that does not trample on persons' First Amendment rights to free speech and political expression, while ensuring all citizens an equal opportunity to serve in elective public office.

District of Columbia Representation in the House

One of the ironies of our congressional scheme under Ex-Con is that the residents of our federal seat, the District of Columbia, do not enjoy representation in our federal legislature. Re-Con addresses this exclusion by providing D.C. a representation in the House apportioned to its population. Statehood for the district is not envisioned by Re-Con because it is a city, joined at the hip with the federal government in ways not shared by any other State. Surgically untwining the two might be possible; the larger question is whether it is advisable. Granting D.C. a representation in the Senate, but without statehood, might be a more practical and elegant solution.

Bi-Monthly Joint Sessions

Under our current system, the House and Senate can seem like parallel universes, without sufficient interaction and cooperation. In fact, other than for a President's yearly state of the union address, they rarely meet in joint session or vote jointly. Re-Con attempts to bring the two bodies into greater contact by requiring that they meet in joint session at least six times a year, on the first Monday of every even-numbered month. As Re-Con's Article V provides, in those joint sessions the President would be required to appear and take questions from the congresspersons, and make whatever statements he or she wishes. Between the bi-monthly joint sessions, the House and Senate may meet separately at any time of their choosing, but are required by Re-Con to maintain a joint ten-person Congressional Conference as a liaison working group.

Impeachment

Impeachment is another occasion in which Re-Con brings the two bodies together to collaborate. Under Ex-Con, impeachment duties are separated: only the House, by a majority vote, can impeach; then the process moves to the Senate, which tries the matter, a two-thirds supermajority required for conviction. One problem with this constitutional regimen is that since the House can initiate an impeachment trial from a low threshold (simple majority), there is a temptation to use impeachment as a partisan axe.

Under Re-Con, either the House or Senate can initiate an impeachment, but the action must be approved by a two-thirds supermajority. Then the two bodies meet jointly to try the impeachment, a two-thirds supermajority of each body being required for conviction. Ex-Con characteristically lists juridical justifications for impeachment (treason, bribery, other high crimes and misdemeanors); Re-Con recognizes that impeachment is an inherently political process (despite use of the word 'trial') that does not require a crime to justify removing someone from high office. Re-Con establishes no standard for impeachment: a person may be impeached for any reason, or for that matter, no reason at all. The only requirement is that two-thirds of both the Senate and the House of Representatives agree.

Disqualification from Future Federal Office

Beyond removal from office, Ex-Con (Article I Section 3) adds a second potential consequence of impeachment: "...disqualification to hold and enjoy any office of honor, trust or profit under the United States...." What "office...under the United States" refers to is unclear. Various passages in Ex-Con distinguish Senators and Representatives from officers, implying that someone impeached and convicted cannot be disqualified from future service in Congress. There is no scholarly consensus (or legal precedent) concerning disqualification from future service as President or Vice President. The most one can safely assume is that "office...under the United States" includes appointive federal statutory offices.

Disqualification has been imposed very rarely, and only on judges. Although Ex-Con requires the agreement of a supermajority of attending Senators for an impeachment conviction and removal from office, the practice has been to further impose disqualification from future federal office by vote of a simple majority. It is widely assumed that the Senate has some discretion in its disqualification power. For example, allowing it to specify which offices are proscribed for an individual; whether the disqualification is permanent, or for a term; and to decide at a future date to reverse its disqualification. Ex-Con however is silent on all these points.

The disqualification power's rare use has helped it avoid scrutiny, but one can easily imagine how the power could be abused. Imagine a high federal officeholder – President, Vice President, judge, justice, cabinet member – who is actively upsetting the status quo, rocking the boat enough to alarm the entire spectrum of entrenched political interests. Let us further imagine that the officeholder is guilty of nothing more than doing his or her job too well, practicing or advocating values of democracy or justice that the political class – while giving those values lip service – is mortally opposed to. Or more mundanely, suppose the target is simply a political rival or enemy of at least a majority of the House, and a supermajority of the Senate. How can Congress use Ex-Con to permanently fix that person's wagon?

Impeachment conviction and disqualification not only removes the undesirable from office, it also prohibits the person from occupying future federal office, possibly forever. The ostracism, whether permanent or for a period of time, is iron-clad: under Ex-Con there is nothing the public can do to reverse the Senate's action. Even the courts lack clear recourse to unwind a disqualification and restore the person's ability to occupy federal office.

Yet federal courts are the only forum where it is possible for disqualification to be lawful, because unlike congressional impeachment 'trials,' the judiciary is where the constitutional guarantee of due process of law resides. Proscriptions against federal officeholding should be considered only under special judicial circumstances, as a punishment relevant to the nature of a crime, after a defendant has undergone a *real* trial, with the protections of due process, and been found guilty. Rights of appeal should encompass both the conviction and any disqualification from federal office.

Senate impeachment trials are by comparison kangaroo courts; their exercise of disqualification violates Ex-Con's Fifth Amendment prohibition against depriving any person "of life, liberty, or property, without due process of law." The *persona non grata* is deprived both of liberty – because he or she has lost the freedom to serve in future federal office – and of property, because an employment ban not only deprives the person of the potential salary and benefits of future federal office, it renders them radioactive, crippling their ability to earn a living outside of government service.

The disqualification clause contradicts another stricture within Ex-Con. Bills of attainder (where a legislature prosecutes, convicts and punishes someone) are twice prohibited by Ex-Con, at both the federal (Article I Section 9) and State (Article I Section 10) levels. One of the traditional categories of punishment imposed by bills of attainder is an employment ban. It may be argued that the purpose of the disqualification clause is preventative, not punitive, but tell that to the person proscribed. It is clearly at best both a prophylactic and a penalty. The disqualification power is another example of Ex-Con's failure to thoroughly purge its legislative scheme of the sort of quasi-judicial powers the English Parliament of its time routinely exercised.

Re-Con does not attach a power of disqualification from federal office to an impeachment conviction; on the contrary, its Article IV Section 6 states that "...Congress shall not impose further penalties or disabilities on any persons impeached and convicted...."

Bicameral Parity

Most of the other divisions of labor between the House and Senate, for example Ex-Con's provision that only the House may initiate spending bills, are set aside. Under Re-Con either body may pass proposals of any kind, and send them to the other body for consideration. Ex-Con gives the powers of ratifying treaties and confirming presidential appointments to the Senate; under Re-Con those responsibilities are shared.

500 Congresspersons

Because the two bodies meet jointly on a regular basis, the number of Representatives is reduced slightly under Re-Con to keep joint-session procedures from becoming unwieldy. While the number of Senators remains the same, the number of Representatives shrinks from 435 to 400, bringing the total number of congresspersons to 500. This small change also simplifies congressional math, when calculating quorums and majorities.

It should be emphasized that under Re-Con votes of the Senate and House are always counted separately, even when the two bodies meet in joint session, with one exception. If the national vote for the Presidency were to result in a tie, Article V Section 1 provides that "...the members of Congress in office at the time of the election shall choose between the tied candidates in special joint session, each Senator and Representative to have one vote." This scenario is of course highly unlikely, given that tens of millions of votes are cast in presidential elections. But if it did happen, Re-Con gives greater weight (four/fifths, or 400 out of 500 total votes) to the House than the Senate, because the distribution of Representatives approximates the distribution of voters.

In the even more unlikely event that Congress's tiebreaking vote also ends in a tie, this is the sole constitutionally-mandated circumstance under Re-Con in which the Vice President breaks a tie vote: "...the Vice President at the time of the general election shall cast the deciding vote, but may not vote for him- or herself." A consequence of restricting the Vice President's tiebreaking mandate to presidential elections is that there is no mechanism in Re-Con for breaking a tie vote in either body. If the Senate or House are evenly split on a vote, that is their problem to work out. However, since "...the Senate and the House of Representatives shall together make the rules by which they cooperate..." (Article IV Section 9), it is possible that the two bodies might agree to offer further tiebreaking responsibilities to the Vice President as the presiding officer in joint sessions of Congress.

Earmarks

One of the least savory aspects of congressional procedure pertains to the larding of bills with extraneous 'earmarks,' designed to please and procure the vote of this or that congressperson. Favor-trading ('logrolling') is a venal tradition in the Congress, that Re-Con attempts to deter by requiring that each proposal or bill pertain to only one subject, defined by its preamble, and that appropriations be separate bills, not add-ons to an omnibus leviathan. Politicians are fond of telling us that we don't want to know how the legislative sausage is made, but since we're paying for the sausage, as well as having to eat and digest its consequences, we need constitutional strictures against larding.

State Recall of Congresspersons

Many States have developed provisions for voters' recall of a State or local elected official, removing someone from office before their term would otherwise end, and replacing them with another. At present the States and their citizens do not have that prerogative when it comes to their federal representatives in Congress.

Re-Con instead provides that a State may recall and replace a member of their congressional delegation, in a procedure conforming to the laws of that State. A State and its citizens should not be stuck with a federal congressperson whom they feel is not representing them in a satisfactory manner, just as a State can now pass laws creating a process for the recall and replacement of a State official who is performing unacceptably.

While Ex-Con does not provide for a State to recall its federal elected officials, it does allow members of Congress to expel one of their own (Article I Section 5). Re-Con removes this ability from Congress. Other than censure, a congressperson is free under Re-Con from official reprisal from his or her colleagues, because that congressperson is not ultimately answerable to other congresspersons. He or she is instead answerable to the State electorate, who alone should have the power of expulsion.

Article V: Federal Executive

The history of the federal executive is one of steadily expanding size and power over the decades. What began as a lightly staffed and tightly circumscribed branch of government has become a metastasizing behemoth.

The presidency has likewise waxed larger, becoming accustomed to an extra-constitutional exercise of powers that properly belong to Congress, the States or the judiciary. Examples of executive overreach are hard to overlook: whether engaging in military conflict without congressional approval, or even prior consultation; usurping legislative authority through executive orders, or secrecy through 'executive privilege;' even the odd and contradictory custom of issuing 'signing statements' that undermine the intent and substance of the very congressional bill just signed into law.

Article V begins by attempting to concisely define a federal executive "which shall be empowered and required to enact, administer, and enforce this Re-Constitution, its amendments, and the laws and actions approved by Congress." This directive is designed to be a short, simple leash: the executive branch is mandated to serve the nation by carrying into effect and upholding federal constitutional and statutory law. Re-Con then offers a few changes to the presidency:

Naturalized Citizen Eligibility

Concerning eligibility and term of office, Ex-Con's Twenty-Second Amendment two-term limit on the presidency is preserved, along with the minimum age (thirty-five). On the other hand, the requirement that the President be a natural-born citizen is abandoned, in favor of a fourteen-year minimum period of citizenship (twice that of Congress) for a naturalized citizen to serve as President or Vice President. In this regard Re-Con aligns with the Framers, who did not actually prohibit a foreign-born citizen from becoming President, so long as the naturalization had occurred by the time Ex-Con was ratified; beyond that, they simply required a minimum fourteen-year U.S. residency (Article II Section 1). This was understandable, as the Framers were attempting to consolidate a new nation and rightly feared foreign conspiracy, especially English revanchism. Those concerns no longer apply.

America has always, and justifiably, branded itself as a beacon for immigrants and land of opportunity. Not only is it fair to offer all qualified citizens an equal opportunity to serve as President or Vice President, it serves the country by accessing a greater talent base. It was argued in the Article I discussion above that naturalized citizens often prize their citizenship more highly because they earned it; it is equally true that naturalized citizens are often our greatest patriots. Wherever possible, Re-Con attempts to increase the value of achieving citizenship, which the ability to reach the highest office in the land certainly does.

Straightforward Remedies for 'Inability' or Vacancy

Ex-Con's Twenty-Fifth Amendment Section 4 provides a mechanism for removing a President for reasons of 'inability.' Unfortunately the process outlined for removing an allegedly incapacitated President is an invitation, if not to a palace coup, at the very least to a protracted constitutional crisis exactly when quick, decisive action might be required. The process is so messy and ill-conceived, we should make a detour to explore its twists and turns.

It starts simply enough, with a letter to Congress from the Vice President and "a majority of either the principal officers of the executive departments or of such other body as

Congress may by law provide," upon which "the Vice-President shall immediately [sic] assume the powers and duties of the office as Acting President." If at a later time the deposed President writes Congress a letter saying no such inability exists, the VP and his co-signers have four days to send a second declaration that the deposed President is indeed "unable to discharge the powers and duties of his office." Then Congress takes over, having two days to convene, and another twenty-one days to decide the issue. A two-thirds supermajority of both houses is required to confirm the deposed President's inability. All of this back-and-forth can easily take a month or more, while a cloud hangs over the country. It has been said that lawyers love a sloppy contract or law, because it gives them plenty to belly up to. In that regard, Ex-Con's Twenty-Fifth Amendment Section 4 is a smorgasbord.

    The prescribed process is so convoluted, it can distract us from an even more ominous aspect of the amendment: the Vice President – second-in-command and beneficiary of the President's removal – is the linchpin of Section 4. Imagine a power-hungry Vice President: all he or she must do is convince a handful of cabinet (or congressional body) members to sign a letter to Congress averring the President's inability. Or imagine the opposite: a slavishly loyal Vice President, who wouldn't act to remove the President no matter how obvious the inability.
    In any case, nothing happens without the Vice President's participation. Yet the Vice President – whether usurper or toady or somewhere in-between – is the *last* person who should be given control over a process to remove an allegedly incapacitated President.

    Re-Con instead offers a straightforward remedy for an incapacitated President that is procedurally indistinguishable from that of impeachment. As discussed above, under Re-Con all it takes to replace a President is a two-thirds supermajority of both the Senate and the House. It doesn't matter whether it's for political misdeeds, criminal predicates, moral transgressions, or mental or physical incapacity. The process can be drawn out through prolonged argument and testimony and presentation of evidence, or as need may be, a quick and decisive vote that replaces a President who obviously can no longer do the job, for whatever reason.

Another circumstance in which decisive action is required is if both the President and Vice President die at the same time, or suffer some other calamity such that both offices lie vacant. Under Re-Con, Congress is to meet in joint session as speedily as possible and vote to appoint a new President. The new President then has the prerogative of appointing his or her Vice President, without the need for congressional approval. This same prerogative obtains when the Vice President assumes office upon removal of the President for any reason. If within two weeks of accession, the new President has not appointed a Vice President, Re-Con provides that Congress shall do so. The goal here is to provide an expedited process whereby a perilous situation can be quickly cured, and the two highest offices reoccupied with as little delay as possible.

Warmaking Powers

Ex-Con gives the power of declaring war to Congress, but you would never know it by our recent history. Re-Con attempts to return warmaking authority to Congress by setting a higher bar for a declaration of war (two-thirds supermajority of both houses) and a lower bar for setting the rules for conducting a war, or for declaring an end to a war (simple majority of both houses). In none of these votes may the President veto Congress's decision. Treaties and agreements with foreign countries are ratified by a two-thirds supermajority of both houses.

Presidential Powers Solely Executive

Ex-Con gives certain powers to the Presidency that impinge upon those of other branches of government. For example, the President is presently given powers to convene (and even adjourn) Congress, decisions which should be left solely to the legislators themselves. Similarly, Ex-Con gives the President an ability to reprieve or pardon anyone convicted of a federal crime, a power that has been so broadly interpreted by a President as allowing him to *immunize* an ex-President against possible future criminal prosecution. However interpreted, powers of reprieve and pardon deprive the judicial branch of its sole authority to render judgments and determine criminal punishment. The powers over the legislative and judicial branches that Ex-Con gives to the Presidency are historical vestiges of monarchic prerogatives, and are disavowed within Re-Con.

Article VI: Federal Judiciary

While Re-Con offers changes to the federal legislature and executive that are relatively minor in nature, leaving Congress and the Presidency in recognizable form, the same cannot be said for the federal judiciary. Instead of the unitary federal court system we now have, Re-Con recommends a bicameral judiciary, with two parallel federal court systems performing a division of duties.

As under Ex-Con, the Supreme Court and lower federal courts would continue to try criminal and civil cases and hear appeals. A second court system, headed by a new High Court of Review, along with newly-established lower federal review courts, would be created to examine the constitutionality of our laws, and the lawfulness of governmental actions. The federal review courts would also handle disputes between the States, between States and the federal government, and between branches of the federal government.

Government Gone Wild

The starting point for understanding the rationale behind this recommendation is to examine a systematic deficiency in our current judicial framework, which puts the people at an unfair advantage in dealings with our government at all levels. This judicial fly-in-the-ointment has caused us to lose control over those who govern us. Let's walk through how and why we are forever playing catchup with the actions of our own government.

Any government agency, whether legislative or administrative, at any level (local, state or federal), can pass a law, resolution, rule, order, or take virtually any action it chooses at any time. Prior judicial restraint on government action does not effectively exist. Suppose (this shouldn't strain anyone's imagination) that the law or action is flagrantly unconstitutional or otherwise unlawful, or unfair, discriminatory, unwarranted, cruel, even nonsensical. When this happens, as it does all the time, what can you do?

Under current practice, the law or action stands until it can be enjoined or overturned in court. The courts are crowded with cases, so there are inevitable delays and continuances. It can be expensive to bring a case against the government, and lawyers are not always eager to 'sue city hall,' so persons of limited means (often those most oppressed by the government action) haven't the wherewithal to proceed. And if they do, the government has our tax money to lavish on its defense.

In addition, our civil law usually requires that someone be damaged first, as a cause of action, in order to bring suit against a government agency. We even have misbegotten judicial interpretations that give a so-called 'qualified immunity' to individuals in government for their official actions. This effectively encourages them to act as they please, confident that they will not be held personally liable for their actions, or in many cases aggressively defended at public expense by the agency employing them.

The upshot of this system is that people suffer under unconstitutional laws and unwarranted, even criminal, government actions for years without effective recourse. It has encouraged a government-gone-wild attitude among public officials, knowing that only on the rarest of occasions are their activities actually stopped.

Federal Review Courts: A Check on Government

A system of federal review courts, whose primary purpose is to examine the constitutionality of our laws, or the lawfulness of governmental actions, whenever they are credibly drawn into question, whether or not anyone has been damaged by them, or even before they have been enacted, would have a number of beneficial effects. Most importantly, it would create a judicial institution specifically designed to check and balance the powers of the other two branches of government, at all levels. Federal review courts would also have jurisdiction over disputes *between* government branches and levels. An immediate, system-wide effect would be to put all public officials on notice that they are on a much shorter leash than the current system provides.

A Curb on Presidential Abuse of the Executive Branch

Federal review courts offer a solution to a vexing flaw in our government: if "All executive branch appointees serve at the pleasure of the President" (Re-Con Article II), yet federal law enforcement is within the executive branch, what is to stop a President (or attorney general, who also serves at the pleasure of the President) from firing anyone who might be investigating the chief executive, or anyone else the President doesn't want investigated?

Ex-Con's Article II Section 2 vests the President with power to appoint "ambassadors, other public ministers and consuls, judges of the supreme court, and all other officers of the United States, whose appointments are not herein otherwise provided for, and which shall be established by law." A proviso then follows: "But the Congress may by law vest the appointment of such inferior officers, as they think proper, in the president alone, in the courts of law, or in the heads of departments."

Ex-Con's language indicates that the President shall appoint *principal* officers, while Congress shall decide who will appoint *inferior* officers, but the distinction is not defined. With each inferior office appointment, Congress can give that authority either to the President, or the courts, or the head of the department in question "as they think proper." Congress has vested the appointment of inspectors general in the

President; the appointment (and removal) of special counsels (aka special prosecutors) is vested in the attorney general.

The problem with Ex-Con's Article II Section 2 isn't simply that the language is imprecise. More importantly, the passages refer solely to *appointments*, not *removals* from office. That matter is unaddressed in Ex-Con, leaving by default the presumption that – like it or not – the ultimate power of removing executive branch officers does rest with the chief executive. Congress has legislated otherwise in the case of special counsels, although the laundry list of vague causes for dismissal renders them little more than at-will employees of the attorney general.

And that brings us back to where we started. Under Ex-Con, Congress has the power to approve (or reject) appointments, and can decide in some cases who gets to make the appointments. Congress has even reached so far as to specify *which* executive may remove special counsels. But executive branch power to remove executive branch appointees remains untouched.

As a result, Congress has fecklessly nibbled away at this conundrum any which way it can. It has required that certain executive branch appointees serve for a nominal term, although they are still essentially at-will employees. If inspectors general are fired by the President, or special counsels by the attorney general, or they are obstructed in their duties, Congress attempts to investigate, or legislate further requirements. But the greater the effort, the clearer its futility. Our separation-of-powers doctrine generally prohibits the federal legislature from overriding executive branch firings.

Federal review courts wouldn't cut the gordian knot, but they would have a number of tools to inhibit a President or attorney general attempting to cashier any unwelcome investigators. Under Re-Con, federal review courts could act immediately to hold any executive action in abeyance while a judicial enquiry ensued into the circumstances and purported cause of dismissal. During that time, the unwelcome investigator's work could continue. Public testimony could be taken from all parties involved. Presidential invocation of executive branch privilege, to keep executive branch members from testifying, could be treated as contempt and factored into the review court's judgment.

Other provisions within Re-Con could further inhibit executive branch preemption of investigations. Mandatory bi-monthly appearances before Congress would be a very public opportunity to question the President on any perceived obstruction or suspicious firings. Re-Con's streamlined impeachment process provides another disincentive.

All branches of government have inherent powers of investigation (i.e., fact-finding); in our current system, judicial investigative prerogatives are largely untapped, a deficiency federal review courts are designed to remedy. Equally, all members of the public have an inherent right to search for the truth in any matter. Exercise of their right of referendum under Re-Con would be a democratically-direct corrective to executive misbehavior.

Sovereign Legal Immunity

Another benefit resulting from the creation of federal review courts is to constitutionally eliminate the possibility of our government claiming sovereign immunity from American complainants in court. Sovereign immunity – the venerable conceit that government can be taken to court, only if it consents – is not mentioned in Ex-Con; it is instead assumed, as a carryover from monarchy, that a sovereign can be sued in court only if he (or she, or it) agrees.

Most countries have doctrines of sovereign immunity in one form or another, although the circumstances under which governments can claim immunity from domestic suit have been narrowing, as they have in the United States. It is nevertheless not good enough to continue to erode the doctrine; it is so pernicious, it should be made constitutionally impossible.

The Citizenry as Sovereign

Under our system, it is the American citizens who are supposed to be the sovereign power, not any government institution per se. As the Declaration of Independence envisioned, government is *a creation of* the people. If government is indeed to be our creature, then every State and federal authority must always be legally answerable to the people. There should exist no circumstances in which government can avoid judicial scrutiny of the laws it passes, and the actions it takes. Re-Con provides that guarantee through a new system of federal review courts.

Re-Con's repudiation of sovereign immunity is designed to apply internally, within the United States. All branches and levels of American government would retain sovereign legal immunity from any foreign complainants, whether individuals, organizations, corporations or governments. Moreover, the United States retains a general, blanket sovereign immunity on all matters concerning foreign entities, notwithstanding any supranational agreements, which as a sovereign nation we are free to terminate at any time.

Re-Con would bring other needed changes to the federal judiciary:

Increased Independence from Congress and the President

One of the problems with Ex-Con is that it gives Congress and the President powers over the judiciary they should not have. For example, it empowers Congress to create lower federal courts; under Re-Con, lower court organization would be left to the justices of the Supreme Court and High Court of Review. Ex-Con gives the power of appointment of lower federal court judgeships to the President; under Re-Con, this would be the prerogative of the justices, respectively, of the two high courts. Ex-Con gives the power of setting judicial salaries to Congress; under Re-Con, compensation is constitutionally mandated as multiples of average nationwide ordinary income. Salaries of Congress, the President, Vice President and other executive officers are similarly defined.

Such measures reflected the Framers' fear of an unchecked federal judiciary. But they pale in comparison to Ex-Con's Article III Section 2 'exceptions' clause, which gives Congress an astonishing – and rarely exercised – control over the Supreme Court: "...the Supreme Court shall have appellate jurisdiction, both as to law and fact, with such exceptions, and under such regulations as the Congress shall make."

In other words, Ex-Con empowers Congress to legislate which cases (or types of cases) the Supreme Court shall hear on appeal, as well as 'regulate' (i.e., make the rules) by which permitted cases shall be heard and decided. Nothing in the exceptions clause or the rest of Article III places limitations on Congress's power to excise and regulate the Supreme Court's appellate docket: it can restrict the Court from reviewing any particular case, or any particular type of case; it can disallow any particular subjects or topics from review, or cases involving any particular individuals or entities. For those cases that the Supreme Court is permitted to hear on appeal, Congress can also regulate its conduct, for example by legislating special rules of procedure.

The exceptions clause is as open-ended as it is outlandish. We can only be grateful that – at least to this date – its destructive potential has not been widely exploited. But there it is, lying in wait.

Re-Con explicitly eliminates the possibility of any congressional control over the dockets of the Supreme Court or High Court of Review: "The Supreme Court, and lower federal case courts under its direction that it creates as necessary, shall hear and decide *all* [emphasis added] federal criminal and civil trials and appeals." And further: "The High Court of Review, and lower federal review courts under its direction that it creates as necessary, shall have authority to review and determine the constitutionality of *all* [emphasis added] laws, and the lawfulness of *all* [emphasis added] actions, of federal, state, and local government, except the judiciary, where deciding criminal and civil trials and appeals."

Mandatory Retirement Age

Justices and judges are appointed without term, and hold their positions under good behavior (subject to impeachment) as under Ex-Con. Re-Con mandates retirement, however, at the age of eighty.

Lifetime judicial appointments have created problems. There have been painful examples through our history of judges and justices continuing to serve when their mental capacities are obviously diminished, or their physical deterioration cannot cope with the rigors of the job. It is a commonplace that judges and justices delay a desired retirement simply because the administration that would nominate their successor is not to their political liking. The result is someone on the bench who would prefer not to be there, but is placeholding until political circumstances change. An age limit lends a predictability to the process, and gives jurists a much-deserved retirement.

Article VII: The States

A distinction that has become standard in political dialogue is that the federal government has *powers*, while the States have *rights*. Re-Con does not observe this distinction, instead defining rights as something only individual persons possess. All government entities, from a nation itself down to the local sewer authority, have powers. Re-Con's Article III defines a State's authority very simply, as all matters that are internal to it.

Much of Article VII recapitulates State powers or obligations articulated in Ex-Con, and will not be rehearsed here. Discussion will be confined to Re-Con's divergences from the boilerplate.

Federal Impartiality Toward the States

Re-Con expressly prohibits the federal government from showing partiality toward one State, or against another. Presidents and executive agencies sometimes play favorites, or punish troublesome States, especially when it comes to federal fiscal largesse. This provision gives States a constitutional cause of action in a federal court of review against unequal treatment.

Federal Financing of Federal Mandates

Under Re-Con, if the federal government mandates an action on the part of a State, it must provide funding sufficient for the mandate's fulfillment. This might seem like common sense, but under our current system States are often left to foot the bill for a federal requirement.

State Powers of Self-Protection

As in Ex-Con, Re-Con requires that the federal government protect the States from invasion or insurrection, but also specifies a protection from illegal foreign entry. Ex-Con's Article I Section 10 authorizes States to protect themselves if actually invaded, or in imminent danger of invasion. Re-Con broadens this authority, so that a State has authority to act on its own to protect itself from invasion, insurrection or illegal foreign entry, if it finds that the federal government is not fulfilling its requirement.

There are other, more significant contrasts between Ex-Con's and Re-Con's treatments of the relationship between the federal government and the States.

State Powers of Political Innovation

Ex-Con (Article IV Section 4) guarantees to the States "a republican form of government." The assumption has been that 'republican' in that passage means no more than 'non-monarchic,' and is more like a warning against any State that would attempt to revert to anything the federal government considered monarchic or tyrannical. Since the passage arrives on the heels of language requiring States to return fugitive slaves to their owners, 'republican' cannot have any meaning in Ex-Con that we would recognize as resembling a 'thing of the people.'

Re-Con does not restrict the form of government a State may adopt, so long as it does not violate constitutional provisions. Under Re-Con, States may experiment, within constitutional limits, with their form of government. As examples, a State might choose a gubernatorial triumverate, or regional divisions of State authority. The States are indeed laboratories of government, and should have powers to innovate within constitutional bounds.

A Constitutional Mishmash of Fundamental Rights Guarantees

Ex-Con's Bill of Rights only mentions Congress once, in the First Amendment. There is no indication, in the language of its other amendments, that the States are excused from respecting any of the rights expressed. That excusal was belatedly solidified by judicial interpretation, and to this day, the Supreme Court still has not finished the job of fully 'incorporating' the entire Bill of Rights 'against' the States.

This historical aversion to enforcing constitutionally-guaranteed civil rights against the States has had awkward consequences. Ex-Con's Fourteenth Amendment due process clause is a verbatim restatement of the due process clause of the Fifth Amendment, on the assumption that the latter did not apply to the States. The Fourteenth Amendment's privileges and immunities clause largely recapitulates language from Ex-Con's Article IV Section 2, in an attempt to clean up what Article IV meant by "the several states," a bone constitutional scholars are still gnawing on. In any case, the Fourteenth Amendment prohibits the States from abridging "the privileges or immunities of the citizens of the United States," but *rights* are not specifically mentioned.

As a result the only reason First Amendment rights (freedom of religion, speech, press, assembly, petition for redress) are recognized as applying to the States is by judicial interpretation, even though the language specifically prohibits only *Congress* from violating these rights, and the Fourteenth Amendment fails to mention State protection of federal rights, instead referring to federal privileges and immunities. If one delves into the writings of the Fourteenth Amendment's authors (and opponents), it is evident that they generally understood 'rights' to be encompassed within 'privileges and immunities,' and the three terms are slurred together often enough. But the equal protection and due process clauses protect *persons*, while the privileges and immunities clause refers to *citizens*. The differences in wording imply that the States are prohibited from abridging a class of protections (privileges and immunities) that are enjoyed by citizens, but not applicable to all persons. Citizens' federal rights are still left dangling, not mentioned or specifically protected from State violation.

Guarantees of fundamental rights should not depend on scholastic exegesis, especially when we come up empty-handed. There is no explicit language in either the First or Fourteenth Amendments (or elsewhere in Ex-Con) that prohibits the States from violating a citizen's federal civil rights.

It gets worse. The Fourteenth Amendment specifically enjoins the States against denying persons the equal protection of the laws; conspicuous by its absence is any mention of the federal government also being enjoined. The Fourteenth Amendment was composed in the context of tightening control over the southern, recently confederate States, but the failure to include the federal government in the equal protection clause was an unhelpful omission. The Supreme Court solved the problem through 'reverse incorporation,' using for the Fourteenth Amendment the opposite process it felt the need to invent to apply selected provisions of the Bill of Rights against the States.

The overarching point here is that on the most important, fundamental rights that State and federal government *must* guarantee to every person, the language of Ex-Con, from the original text through the Bill of Rights and the Fourteenth Amendment, is woefully unclear. Constitutional assurances of our most basic civil rights have depended on the vagaries of judicial interpretation, which has changed over time and can change again.

Archaisms

Ex-Con's language is littered with other archaisms and inconsistencies. Most of them are of smaller consequence, compared to those treated above. But in a federal constitution, our democratic social contract, any wiggle room on any subject is an invitation for the malefactors among us to willfully misinterpret the text. As a sample of Ex-Con oddities, for which the courts have improvised workarounds (or simply ignored), here are two chestnuts:

Ex-Con's Proof of Treason

Ex-Con's Article III Section 3 requires that a necessary condition for a conviction of treason – other than confession – is that two witnesses testify to the same "overt act." For its time, this language laudably strengthened existing English safeguards for defendants facing a capital charge of treason, with the understanding that such trials can be, as Benjamin Franklin put it, "virulent." "Witness" meant *eyewitness*, so that two people had to testify that they both saw (i.e., witnessed in person) the accused commit the same overt act of treason.

Two eyewitnesses to an 'overt act' is not a realistic condition of proof of treason in the modern world. First, as the Article III treatment above discussed, treason (and its eyewitnessing) can only occur during a war. Second, and more to the modern point, eyewitnessing an overt act isn't how we're likely to catch traitors today. More likely we intercept or trace their furtive communications – e.g., phone or internet – with our enemies. These and other traitorous acts are typically covert, not overt. We don't normally 'witness' such acts: we discover them, usually in the course of an investigation. So under Ex-Con's standard of proof we have to awkwardly classify two investigators as 'witnesses' in order to secure a conviction of treason, when of course they aren't witnesses in the sense that either the Framers, or our contemporary usage, would recognize. And in addition, the surreptitious actions have to be awkwardly classified as overt, again in a sense that our contemporary usage doesn't recognize.

"Excluding Indians Not Taxed"

Ex-Con's Fourteenth Amendment Section 2 details a process for allocating federal Representatives, by counting the number of persons within a State, but then adds "excluding Indians not taxed." This phrase was interpreted as referring to head taxes (capitations), a direct tax on every person still prevalent in the nineteenth century. However, if an Indian was living on a reservation, they were not required to pay the head tax, and according to the Fourteenth Amendment, not counted as within a State's population for the purposes of calculating its representation in Congress.

It took all the way to 1924 before all Native Americans who lived within the States were declared citizens, whether they lived on a reservation or not. Yet this language – "excluding Indians not taxed" – is still in Ex-Con. Its meaning has been less than clear from the outset, and it makes a connection between taxpaying and inclusion in a census that we do not countenance. We are now in an era where head taxes no longer exist, but income taxes do. Yet if we take the phrase literally, at face value, there are lots of Native Americans (many children, elderly, unemployed, for example) who are not taxed. Are we to exclude untaxed Indians from the census? Of course not. So we do the right thing, count everyone in the census, and ignore the language of the Fourteenth Amendment.

Improvisation Masquerading as Interpretation

It has become routine for us to ignore outdated constitutional passages, or to perform sophistries that bend their meaning, in order to cope with the shortcomings of the text. These improvisations are understandable: we must have law to adjudicate cases, whether we have a Constitution that guides us or not. But does it need to be pointed out that there is a danger in making it up as we go along, while pretending to be interpreting our supreme legal document?

Article VIII: Conduct of Elections

Although elections are the centerpiece of representative democracy, the Framers eschewed mandating the nuts and bolts of the electoral mechanism, leaving the details to the States. As a result, whatever can go wrong in an American election, has gone wrong, many times over. Re-Con attempts to restructure and tighten the process, with the understanding that for some there will be always be a temptation, given the opportunity, to corrupt elections and subvert the will of the people.

Ex-Con (Article I Section 4) grants States discretion in the "times, places and manner of holding elections" for Congress, which may in some respects "make or alter such regulations." The upshot of this passage is that States and their localities have largely managed their own electoral affairs, leaving a hodgepodge of local practice that has fallen prey to every imaginable abuse.

Uniform Electoral Standards and Practices

The first corrective Re-Con applies to elections is to constitutionally mandate that Congress maintain uniform standards and practices across all electoral jurisdictions, nationwide. Uniform electoral procedures are intended to guarantee voters the equal protection of their right to vote, and to have their votes accurately counted.

One contemporary example of how haywire local control of elections can go involves the widespread use of electronic devices and databases in the conduct of elections. Whether it is voter rolls, registration forms, signature records, or most importantly actual vote tabulations and results, it can be safely assumed that any election-related networks connected to the internet are hackable. For that reason all electoral information and equipment should be 'air-gapped,' that is, disconnected from any external information network. Of course air-gapping is not a panacea: we've had a long history of old-school ballot-stuffing and voter suppression before the internet ever came along. But we can avoid a new level of electoral irregularities if we make certain that all votes are recorded on a physical ballot, which can be hand-counted (and re-counted) in the inevitable event a tabulating machine malfunctions, even if it is air-gapped. In any case, we should operate on the prudent assumption that all virtual, non-physical electoral records, and especially ballots, can never be made free from error or secure from manipulation.

Re-Con's Article VIII Section 1 includes a number of specific election-related strictures:

Gerrymandering

Gerrymandering of districts has been a loathsome political exercise throughout our history, becoming ever more precise and targeted with modern technological improvements in compiling exhaustive personal information about voters. Re-Con takes district-drawing out of politicians' hands, and assigns it to ad-hoc non-partisan citizens' commissions, with a mandate to create competitive, compact districts.

Judging Results and Resolving Disputes

In Ex-Con's Article I Section 5, each house of Congress "shall be the judge of the elections, returns and qualifications of its own members." Re-Con goes in the opposite direction, prohibiting any public elective body from judging the results of elections to its positions. The sitting members of a body have the most to gain (or lose) from its own elections, making them the least reliably fair judges of the outcomes.

Re-Con further requires that disputes concerning the results of elections be resolved at the same level of government. This protection is designed to prohibit a higher level of government (state over local, or federal over state) from taking over the handling of an election dispute from a lower level.

Incumbency

Incumbents are prohibited from using their public office, or its resources, to campaign for or against any candidates. That includes themselves, if running for re-election.

Section 2 of Article VIII first establishes standard calendar dates for elections and terms of office, but then focuses on the obligations of public officials.

Public Officials Acknowledged as Our Fiduciaries

Typical oaths of office emphasize loyalty to Ex-Con, or to the United States. What they conspicuously lack is an acknowledgment that public office involves a fiduciary obligation to one's constituents. Re-Con would require of the newly elected that they promise to represent the voters' interests *as their fiduciary*. Let's unpack what that means, and how it can help to reverse the upside-down relationship between the public and government officials.

A *fiduciary* is someone who holds a special relationship of *trust* with another person, known as the *principal*, to act on their behalf and represent their interests. The crucial part of this relationship is that the fiduciary promises in a certain activity to represent the interests of persons other than themselves. Examples of fiduciaries in our society are lawyers, accountants, realtors, negotiators, corporate directors, union officers, executors, trustees, etc.

What is not equally recognized – either in the public mind or the courts – is that government officials, elected or appointed, likewise have a fiduciary duty to represent the interests of their constituents. This despite American law long recognizing that fact: our century-old federal Uniform Fiduciaries Act cited "public officers" as an example of a fiduciary when defining the term on its very first page.

To understand a fiduciary's duties, we should first examine how strictly a fiduciary relationship is treated in an ordinary non-political context, then contrast it to how public officials routinely violate their fiduciary obligations to us.

Imagine that you are negotiating with another party for the purchase of something substantial, say, a piece of real estate. You have a realtor representing you, and the seller has one as well. Each realtor has a fiduciary responsibility to represent the interests of his or her client, interests that should be understood to be distinct and different from their own, their counterpart realtor, or the counterpart's principal. In the course of the negotiation, it would clearly be inappropriate for one realtor to offer or provide any material benefit to the other, or for either principal to offer benefit to their counterpart's realtor. Imagine if the seller secretly offered or gave your realtor money, in return for your realtor convincing you to pay more for the property. Or likewise, if you offered or gave the seller's realtor money, in return for the realtor convincing the seller to take less for the property. Even a small benefit, such as one realtor picking up a lunch tab for the other, could be construed as an inducement to act against a client's interests. Any exchange of benefit between opposing fiduciaries, or between a principal and an opposing fiduciary, in the course of a negotiation is a violation of fiduciary duty.

Now let's take a look at an analogous political situation. Imagine a committee in a State legislature that is negotiating a contract with (as examples) a labor union or a corporation. In this negotiation, the committee member is representing the public as its fiduciary, and the union or corporate officer is representing its members or shareholders as their fiduciary. The two fiduciaries – the legislator and the union/corporate officer – should not provide or offer each other benefit. If they did, it could be construed as a bribe, an attempt to corruptly influence the outcome of the negotiation. The word we use for such an outcome is a *sweetheart* contract, where one fiduciary has been corruptly induced to unfaithfully represent the interests of his or her clients – to betray their trust – shortchanging them in return for the fiduciary receiving personal benefit.

Once the role of a legislator as our negotiator is spelled out like that, it's clear where this line of reasoning is going. Isn't it routine for a labor union, or a corporation, to make campaign contributions to the legislator? If direct contributions are prohibited, they can be funneled through different types of political action committees, soft money, flocks of 'individual' contributions, etc. A super PAC can spend without limit in support of an elected official, so long as a presumed 'independence' is maintained.

In our political world, wouldn't it be seen as remiss of the union or corporation if they *didn't* contribute – directly or otherwise – to each and every legislator (and political party) who had anything to say about the outcome of the negotiation? And if contributions and support didn't succeed, to remind recalcitrant legislators that the union or corporation can contribute to and work very hard for their electoral opponents, next time around?

Yet this is considered entirely legal. The people's fiduciary is given massive financial assistance (or the credible threat of an unseating) by the very entities he or she is negotiating against, and *voilà!* we have contracts with government employees or corporations that are extreme examples of sweetheart contracts. On the union side, under-funded defined-benefit pension packages are so lavishly expensive going forward, the day is coming when we can't possibly pay them. On the corporate side, the government signs and fulfills contracts that no fiscally sane public officials would ever agree to...unless they were being paid to.

Fiduciary Obligations Concerning Campaign Monies

Re-Con addresses this flouting of fiduciary obligation by requiring that "No elected public official shall accept or fail to return campaign contributions from parties negotiating with, doing business for, or seeking permits or special benefits from any agency of government over which he or she has official influence." That covers campaign monies.

Fiduciary Obligations Concerning Other Private Benefit

But there is always the issue of other private benefit, not specifically campaign-related, corrupting the fiduciary obligations of public officials, both elected and appointed. For this, Re-Con provides that "It shall be a criminal offense for citizens to accept or knowingly receive any gift, offering or compensation, or otherwise profit beyond their lawfully determined salary and benefits, as a consequence of their public office."

Fiduciary Obligations Concerning Conflicts of Interest

Some conflicts of interest in fulfilling public duties are unavoidable, which Re-Con attempts to mitigate through disclosure and recusal requirements: "All public officials shall disclose any apparent, potential or actual conflicts of interest in fulfilling their public duties, and shall recuse themselves where the conflicts of interest cannot be eliminated."

Self-Dealing

The final passage in Article VIII Section 2 prohibits self-dealing by public officials, with respect to salary and benefits: "No changes in salary or benefits for any public office shall be retroactive, nor apply to the persons legislating or authorizing the changes, during their tenure in office."

While Article VIII Section 1 deals with basic election procedures, and Section 2 with obligations of public officials, Section 3 focuses on the conduct of electoral campaigns. Re-Con charts out a process that departs markedly from current practice, establishing a constitutional framework for electoral campaigning, a subject that Ex-Con does not treat at all. In order to motivate these sweeping changes, it is necessary to strip the essence of a campaign, that culminates in an election, down to what it really is.

Elections Are a Hiring Process

Public office, if nothing else, is a job. The official gets a salary, and has duties. An electoral campaign is like one long involved job application. The voting public is akin to the hiring committee, who ultimately decide at the end of the process which applicant gets the job. Re-Con uses this frank conceptual framework – a job application and selection – to craft an electoral process that the voting public (the hiring committee) has control over, in which anyone can apply for the job, and every applicant is treated fairly.

Contrast that paradigm with what we now have: it's nothing like a fairly conducted job application and selection over which the public has control. To even be considered, almost every applicant for higher office must have powerful sponsors, in the form of one of two political parties and their donors, who stand to benefit from promoting 'their' candidates.

The political parties – not the voting public – design and control the job application process (i.e., the campaign season). They schedule any debates, and decide who will appear on stage. Their control over debates is so thorough, they have not only kept third party candidates from participating in debates, but even attending the event as audience members. In campaigns for the Presidency, they effectively control the primary season, dictating the order the States will go in, and even the manner in which the voting will be conducted (secret ballot or caucus).

Most of us have applied for jobs, oftentimes many applications for many jobs. We know from experience that the application and hiring process is something we have absolutely no control over. We expect that, and would be shocked otherwise. We fill out application forms, take batteries of tests, undergo background checks and psychological evaluations, endure numerous interviews, give urine samples, maybe even take a polygraph. If we do get hired, it's on a probationary basis. Can the reader imagine a job application-and-selection process where the applicant, and the applicant's sponsors, control all the details? Not unless you're thinking of campaigns for public office, where political parties do everything but punch the ballot for you on election day.

The task then is to devise a process whereby the public alone controls the conduct of campaigns, and ensures fairness, so that everyone has an equal opportunity to compete for office. Here is how Re-Con solves the puzzle:

Signature Gathering

The first stage in running for any public office is to qualify for the ballot. Under Re-Con, a prospective candidate would begin by gathering signatures from the voting public within the electoral district. The catch here is that voters can only endorse one prospective candidate per public office, so they must choose carefully.

Pre-Qualification Exam

The ten prospective candidates for an office who gather the most signatures would then be required to "take an objectively-graded written entrance exam, devised by the legislative authority to test the knowledge and judgment of the prospective candidates relevant to the office sought." This pre-qualification exam should not be subjectively graded or interpreted, like an essay test. It should be a fact-based examination of whether prospective candidates have sufficient prior knowledge and understanding of the office they seek, and the duties it requires.

Primary Ballot Qualification and Campaign

The top five test scorers qualify for the primary ballot; they "shall be required to regularly debate one another, and be tested and examined by the public, in a variety of subjects, formats, and venues." When trying to imagine what primary-season paces the public could put the candidates through, think of a TV reality show that is a competition, as so many of them are. The producers of those shows have no trouble thinking up all sorts of entertaining and revealing challenges that help the judges (who may be the viewing audience) determine the winner.

Re-Con envisions primary campaign season activities conducted by the public, where we devise all manner of examining the candidates, with the same creativity and thoroughness employer hiring committees (and TV reality show producers) practice in evaluating their quarry. These activities would not be optional for the candidates; for that reason, and to ensure that no one is discouraged from seeking office through lack of means, they would be conducted at public expense.

News Media Requirement to Disseminate Campaign Information

During the campaign season, Re-Con would mandate two requirements of all news media operating within an electoral jurisdiction. First, that at their expense they broadcast all required candidate events, and disseminate records of those activities, as well as any public statements from the candidates. And second, that all news media at their expense fairly broadcast and disseminate "persons' diverse expressions of support for or opposition to candidates."

Requiring news media – whether TV, radio, print, internet – to keep the public fully informed as campaigns proceed is a small price to pay for the privilege of operating within the United States, using and enjoying our infrastructure, laws and institutional freedoms.

Disempowering Privately-Funded Campaign Advertisements

The media requirement serves a profoundly important ancillary purpose: it would deprive candidates (and their sponsors) with great financial means of the inherent advantage they now possess in our current system. Our system at present allows persons or organizations to spend as much money as they want, advocating independently for or against a candidate or policy. Candidates are allowed to spend as much as they want of their own money on their own campaigns. It is an uncomfortable truth to admit that these allowances are constitutional: political expression is speech, and a strict adherence to our First Amendment requires that we permit such expression without limit. The only remaining limit – to protect against pay-to-play corruption – is how much one can directly contribute to a candidate.

The problem with our system is that it puts candidates of limited means – who cannot buy up all the ad time and space and fill it with expensive content – at an extreme disadvantage. Re-Con mitigates this problem by requiring news media at their expense to provide access to all publicly-mandated campaign events, and to publish all candidate statements, as well as the opinions of supporters and detractors.
This requirement steals the thunder from candidates or sponsors of great means who would attempt to saturate the media with their propaganda. Under Re-Con they must compete with the ubiquitous coverage and record of actual campaign events, candidate statements, and public comments.

The result is that without limiting anyone's free speech, blanket propaganda is de-fanged of its ability to influence the electorate. A candidate may spend limitless money on slick advertisements telling us how great he or she is, or how awful their competitor is, but if we have easy access to all the occasions and information that prove to us otherwise, it won't matter. What a dishonest candidate or advertisement *says* will stand in stark contrast to what the public *knows*, and may just as easily backfire.

General Election

The primary election in July would prune an electoral field from five candidates to two finalists, who then go through the same process for the general election, with more mandated public events and more mandated news media coverage, culminating in a November run-off vote.

Presidential Elections: an Alternative to the Electoral College

The 1787 constitutional convention almost fell apart early on over States' representation in Congress, an issue the Framers resolved (in 'the Great Compromise') by chartering a bicameral legislature where one chamber gave each State – large or small – equal say.

Weeks later, at the very end of the convention, just before a 'committee of style' would retire over a long weekend to compile all they had agreed to into a constitution, the Framers decided the manner of electing the President. They had previously rejected a direct vote of the people as too democratic and favoring the more populous States. They also rejected having Congress choose the President, because it could make the chief executive subordinate to the legislature.

The solution they settled on (Article II Section 1) had echoes of the Great Compromise. On the one hand, each State would have a number of 'electors' equal to its representation in Congress, which favors the larger, more populous States. On the other hand, if no candidate received votes from a majority of electors (which the Framers thought could easily occur), each State regardless of size would have only one vote in the House of Representatives to choose the President. It was also possible that more than one candidate would receive votes from a majority of the electors, since each elector was to vote for two presidential candidates. Whether one or two candidates received votes from a majority of electors, the candidate with the most electoral votes would become the President, and the runner-up the Vice President.

A third eventuality – that two candidates might receive the same numerical majority of elector votes – promptly occurred in the election of 1800. Thomas Jefferson and Aaron Burr ran on the same party ticket, with the plan that one party elector would vote for someone other than Burr, so Jefferson would receive one more vote and become President. Through a comedy of errors the scheme neglected to happen, causing Jefferson and Burr to tie; the issue then went to the House of Representatives, which deadlocked for *thirty-five* ballots. The impasse was finally broken through plenty of arm-twisting and horse-trading by Alexander Hamilton, who despised Jefferson less than he did Burr. The congressional fiasco was so excruciating it resulted in the Twelfth Amendment, which provided that each elector would vote once for a President and once for a Vice President.

In any iteration, the system that came to be known as the Electoral College made presidential selection a State-by-State process, where each State appoints its own electors. Ex-Con doesn't restrict the range of an elector's choices, beyond a requirement that at least one vote be cast for someone who is not a resident of the elector's State. Such freedom of choice not only means that electors' votes don't need to correspond with the actual votes of their State's electorate for different presidential candidates; it also means that an elector can vote for *anyone,* even persons who aren't candidates.

The Framers devised the Electoral College because they wanted the States – through their electors – to choose the President. They also left it to the States to decide how, and to what degree, their electors would reflect the will of their voters. The States and their electors thereby became oddly uncontrolled intermediaries between the people's votes and the presidential selection, as they are today.

Direct National Vote

Re-Con's Article VIII Section 4 presents a method for conducting presidential elections that bears no resemblance to Ex-Con's Electoral College framework. The power the States now have in selecting the President is rejected in favor of a direct national vote. A presidential election is the only time we all vote together, as a people, for the same public office. If we are to call ourselves a democracy, in any meaningful sense of the word, a nationwide election choosing the person who will occupy the highest office in the land must accurately reflect the will of the people. Under Re-Con the States (and the District of Columbia) do play a new and enhanced role in the preliminary stages of a presidential election, while playing no role in the final presidential vote.

It should be observed that while we routinely refer to our country as a nation, and don't blink at the word 'national' being adapted to name our government seat's major league baseball team, those words are conspicuously absent from Ex-Con. The Framers were exceedingly careful to maintain that they were creating an enhanced federal – but not a national – government. Their consistent reference to our country as the United States was meant literally, as a coalition of sovereign States who created the federal government, and retained control over their creation. Control over a State was reserved to its people, the ultimate sovereign power.

Under Ex-Con, however, the people's sovereign power ends at a State's border. There is no constitutional provision – other than peaceable assembly and petition for redress of grievances – for the American citizenry from different States to act together to check the power of States acting together through the federal government. Without the people having any collective sovereignty corresponding to the collective sovereignty the States themselves enjoy through the federal government, we are politically hobbled. Under Ex-Con we can only check our own State – but not federal – power.

In contrast, Re-Con provides four avenues through which the entire American citizenry can together exercise direct sovereignty over their federal government: general presidential elections, and plebiscites deciding referendums, constitutional ratification and amendments. These four specific contexts are the only instances in which Re-Con employs the word 'national,' empowering the citizenry as a whole to have the final say over the federal government and the States it comprises.

Presidential Primary Elections

Re-Con's presidential primary campaign season begins in the same fashion as primary seasons for any other elective office, with signature gathering of eligible voters in the State of their residence. While Re-Con prescribes a one-year minimum State residency for members of Congress, minimum residency requirements for candidates to participate in a State's presidential primary are left up to that State, and thus may differ from State to State.

For each State, as in other elective offices, the ten persons who gather the most signatures endorsing their presidential candidacies are required to take an objectively-graded entrance exam. The five highest scorers qualify for that State's July presidential primary, and like candidates for other offices, "shall be required to regularly debate one another, and be tested and examined by the public, in a variety of subjects, formats, and venues."

Presidential Secondary Elections

The highest presidential primary vote-getter from each State would then move on to a secondary election, held two months later, in September. The secondary election would be divided into five regions. Each region would comprise ten States, except for the Southeast region, which would include ten States and the District of Columbia. The ten (or eleven) presidential primary winners would together go through a second wave of public examination, culminating in the September presidential 'secondaries.'

Presidential General Election

The winners of the five regional secondaries are now through to the general November election. For the last two months, they undergo another publicly-run and publicly-broadcast grilling. The highest vote-getter in the general election becomes the President; the runner-up becomes the Vice President.

Runner-Up as Vice President

This provision departs from current practice, where presidential and vice-presidential nominees are on the same 'ticket' (invariably meaning the same political party), campaigning and serving together. The perceived advantage is that the two 'running mates' are presumed to have a non-adversarial relationship, that will lend itself to cooperative executive leadership.

In actual practice a presidential nominee often chooses a running mate from among those who were defeated in their party's primary battles. Those contests are no less viciously conducted than the general election; and in any case, the existence of acrimony is just as possible within a political party as it is across party lines.

By having the runner-up in the general election become the Vice President, Re-Con assumes and welcomes a rivalry between the two highest officeholders. The only specific duty that Re-Con assigns the Vice President is to preside over Congress in joint session, and as explained above, cast the deciding vote in the extremely unlikely event that both the voting public and Congress deadlock in their choice of President. Nevertheless, presiding over Congress in joint session is not a ceremonial responsibility, and can wield significant influence under Re-Con. The Vice President would hold the gavel in the mandated bi-monthly joint sessions of Congress, when the President is required to appear and take questions, as well as during all impeachment trials not involving the President or Vice President. If Congress decides to meet in joint session to vote to override a veto, or declare a war (or its rules or cessation), those occasions would provide the Vice President even more opportunities to preside and exercise influence. If the Vice President was not entirely of like mind with the President on matters entertained in joint sessions (which is predictable), a salutary check on presidential power is available to the second-in-command.

The overwhelming reason the runner-up should be the Vice President is because he or she was the nation's second choice, and in the event the President leaves office early, the country has its next-best choice assume power. By coming in second place, the Vice President more than anyone else has earned the privilege of being second-in-line to the Presidency.

Rank-Order Voting

Re-Con's Article VIII Section 5 mandates rank-order voting for presidential primary, secondary and general elections. Each voter on a presidential ballot can list up to three names, for a first, second and third choice. The voter's first choice gives that candidate three points; the second choice two points; and the third choice one point. Each choice must be for a different candidate, and the candidate with the most points wins the election.

Rank-order voting can produce some unusual results. Under Re-Con, someone might win the presidency by being everyone's second choice. The candidate who receives the most first-choice votes, but doesn't win the election, would most likely come in second and serve as Vice President. The wider fields that Re-Con prescribes (five candidates in a primary, ten in a secondary, and five in the general election) give voters more say over the outcome. A voter may have their favorite, but in case he or she doesn't win, the voter has a hand in who else might prevail. The extra choices also give voters the chance to cross party lines, by voting a mixed presidential ticket.

A consequence of rank-order voting is that less extreme candidates tend to do better, because they usually appeal to a wider range of voters. It also encourages civility: a caustic candidate predictably turns off a wide swath of the electorate, and may not appear as any of a voter's three choices. Candidates of like mind might find it in their interests to endorse one another, or even campaign together, forming cooperative slates. In a variety of ways, rank-order voting creates a gravitational field that pulls presidential candidates toward the middle.

Article IX: Citizens' Power of Referendum

Re-Con's Article VIII treats elections for public office, which are a form of *indirect*, or representative, democracy. Some States have forms of more *direct* democracy, where citizens can assert electoral power over their government apart from the periodic election of representatives. These more direct democratic controls have assumed three basic forms:

1. the ability to recall and replace elected public officials during their term;

2. the ability to propose a law and directly vote on it (ballot measure or initiative);

3. the ability to *referend* an action or law of government, rendering it null and void.

Concerning the first form of direct democracy, Re-Con (Article IV Section 8) provides that States may recall and replace their federal Representatives and Senators. Both Ex-Con and Re-con have provisions for Congress to impeach a President or Vice President, among other federal public officials.

The people have the equivalent of the second power (ballot measure/initiative) on the federal level through their power of constitutional amendment, discussed below.

Re-Con prescribes the third power of direct democracy – the referendum – on the federal level in the form of a national plebiscite. Federal review courts have been recommended in Re-Con so that the judicial branch, if a plausible prima facie argument is made, can proceed to examine the constitutionality of a law or the lawfulness of a governmental action. But what if the problem isn't the law's constitutionality, or the action's lawfulness? What if the law or action is simply ill-advised, or unreasonable, or even monstrous, yet somehow avoids violating constitutional or statutory provisions? Or alternatively, suppose that the federal review courts wrongly uphold (or perhaps refuse to even review) an unconstitutional law, or unlawful governmental action? What can we do then?

Re-Con provides that if twenty-six of the States – either through a vote of a State legislature or a State ballot measure – initiate a referendum on a government law or action, it would then be held in abeyance, without effect, while Congress schedules a national plebiscite to decide the matter. The District of Columbia is not given power to share in the initiation of a referendum, but its voters would participate in the plebiscite. Majority approval by the voters would reverse the law or action, rendering it null and void.

Article X: Citizens' Power of Ratification
Article XI: Citizens' Power of Amendment

Re-Con's final two Articles can be considered together, because their provisions mirror each other. In order to ratify or amend Re-Con, two-thirds (thirty-four) of the States would need to authorize a national plebiscite. Proposed amendment language would need to be exactly the same for all authorizing States. As with the power of referendum, the District of Columbia would not have authorizing power, but its voters would participate in the plebiscite. Majority approval by the voters would be required both for constitutional ratification and for amendments.

AFTERWORD

SWEEPINGS FROM THE CUTTING ROOM FLOOR

A constitution, as our nation's democratic social contract, can only be a framework, including our most important, fundamental agreements. Plenty of good ideas simply do not rise to the level of constitutional significance. Perhaps the idea can be inferred from language within a constitution. Or maybe it's something that might work in the future, but today's populace isn't ready to consider just yet.

Here are a few ideas that didn't make the constitutional cut, for one reason or another.

State Secession

Re-Con expressly prohibits a State from seceding. Our nation has permanent scar tissue on this subject, and any suggestion of a State's power to secede is greeted with derision. The issue is beyond debate. Case closed.

Or is it? Can anyone believe in the legitimacy of the United States of America, if we hold that secession can never, under any circumstances, be justified? Our nation was founded on an act of secession, against the world's premier power. The colonists' motives in parting ways with England were a mixed bag, from pecuniary to principled. The mother country had many admirable qualities. Yet most of us revere the creation of our nation not just as a noble act, thoroughly justified, but as a sea change in the history of the world.

The conclusion is unavoidable: secession can be warranted by circumstance. If our federal government became a fascist regime, taking over and destroying our republic, one cannot pronounce in advance that States would not be justified in seceding and opposing it. Most of us agree that it was wrong of the southern States to attempt to secede, because their reason for doing so (preserving slavery) was evil. But would we feel the same sense of condemnation if the northern States had seceded from the Union, in order to wash their hands of slavery, as many abolitionists advocated in the antebellum era?

Re-Con does not allow for State secession not because it is never an acceptable course of action, but because it is an *extra-constitutional* action that can only be evaluated by the circumstances surrounding it. Justifiable contexts cannot be defined in advance. But if they ever occur, we will need a new constitution. Until then, secession is prohibited.

Income Inequality

Re-Con addresses economic issues only insofar as they affect legal and political fairness, defined as equal opportunity. A person of lesser means in our society has less opportunity for justice in the courts, or for achieving elective office. These inequities, although we've become inured to them, should be inimical to our values. Money should not be a factor in how much 'justice' one receives, or whether one can fairly compete for public office. Re-Con offers ways to correct these wrongs.

The underlying issue is however not addressed. We live in a society with wealth disparities so deep, they're difficult to fathom. A person making a six-figure salary in today's America, who saved every penny of their income, would take about *two million years* [not a misprint] to accumulate the wealth of today's richest American. And this almost unimaginable gulf between the rich and the rest of us exists under conditions of scarcity, where the lower strata of society lack the most basic provisions: adequate food, clothing, shelter, medicine.

There is a straightforward way to attack the problem: an income cap. The closest we've come to that solution in the past is having the highest tax brackets attempt to capture virtually all of a person's income above a certain level. Tax avoidance by the rich matched the aggressiveness of the tax brackets, so our gaping wealth chasm didn't narrow all that much.

Policy paradigms addressing wealth disparity continue to follow that general pattern: wherever possible, take the excessive wealth in the form of a tax, and recycle the revenue back to help the disadvantaged. Sounds good, but government is a uniquely wasteful instrument for redistribution of wealth: much of the revenue goes toward graft or a boondoggle or an aircraft carrier, not a decent leg-up for the poor.

What if income beyond a certain annual maximum was not taken by the government, but was instead required to be contributed to a charitable cause? Here's some draft language to that effect, found on the cutting room floor:

> "To mitigate financial inequality, annual individual income from any source shall be limited to ten times the national income average for all full-time working adults over the age of 25. Surplus income exceeding that amount shall be donated by the following April 15th to any charitable, non-profit, public-interest cause(s) of the individual's choosing. The individual may donate to any government agency or entity and earmark the spending of the donation.
>
> All donations shall be public record. No surplus income may be donated to any non-charitable, for-

profit, private interest cause(s), including to any political party or to any candidate for or holder of any public office. Stringent criminal penalties shall be enforced for any failure to donate surplus income, or for surplus income donations received by non-charitable, for-profit, private-interest causes.

Surplus annual income shall not be subject to taxation. Capital gains from the sale of a primary personal residence shall not be subject to surplus annual income limits, but shall be subject to taxation. Windfall income may be structured to be received over multiple years."

Equal Protection Against Unequal Public Education

Re-Con requires the States to provide children an education. There is no mention of the quality of the education, because that can't be easily defined. Besides, States with poor educational systems simply make other States more attractive, and their residents vote with their feet. It is in a State's interest to provide a quality education.

The biggest problem with our educational system is that within any State, or county, *or even the same school district*, there can be an alarming difference in the quality of the public schools and the education they provide. Our courts have largely failed to recognize that – especially within a school district sharing the same budget – it is a violation of Ex-Con's Fourteenth Amendment guarantee of equal protection to allow such vastly different standards.

No urban school district can have identical standards for all its facilities, but the differences are breathtaking. Wealthy urban neighborhoods often have schools that resemble cathedrals; the poor neighborhoods, usually peopled by racial minorities, have facilities that are as safe and inviting as a badly-run penitentiary.

Children are *required* to attend school. They have no choice in the matter. And they will in all likelihood, their parents' best efforts notwithstanding, attend their neighborhood school. If the neighborhood is poor, the school will be as well.

Poor children are compelled, with a few exceptions, to attend poor schools, through no fault of their own. The failure of the courts to enforce uniform educational standards across the breadth of a school district or a community is an institutional guarantee that the poor – especially racial minorities – will suffer multi-generational discrimination.

It is axiomatic that any sector of our society whose children receive a substandard education will never achieve social parity. Is this equal protection issue important enough to be specifically addressed in our federal constitution, or should we continue to leave its belated resolution to the courts and legislatures?

APPENDIX

THE CONSTITUTION OF THE UNITED STATES OF AMERICA

Preamble

We the People of the United States, in Order to form a more perfect Union, establish Justice, insure domestic Tranquility, provide for the common defence, promote the general Welfare, and secure the Blessings of Liberty to ourselves and our Posterity, do ordain and establish this Constitution for the United States of America.

Article I Legislative

Section 1

All legislative Powers herein granted shall be vested in a Congress of the United States, which shall consist of a Senate and House of Representatives.

Section 2

1: The House of Representatives shall be composed of Members chosen every second Year by the People of the several States, and the Electors in each State shall have the Qualifications requisite for Electors of the most numerous Branch of the State Legislature.
2: No Person shall be a Representative who shall not have attained to the Age of twenty five Years, and been seven Years a Citizen of the United States, and

who shall not, when elected, be an Inhabitant of that State in which he shall be chosen.

3: Representatives and direct Taxes shall be apportioned among the several States which may be included within this Union, according to their respective Numbers, which shall be determined by adding to the whole Number of free Persons, including those bound to Service for a Term of Years, and excluding Indians not taxed, three fifths of all other Persons. The actual Enumeration shall be made within three Years after the first Meeting of the Congress of the United States, and within every subsequent Term of ten Years, in such Manner as they shall by Law direct. The Number of Representatives shall not exceed one for every thirty Thousand, but each State shall have at Least one Representative; and until such enumeration shall be made, the State of New Hampshire shall be entitled to chuse three, Massachusetts eight, Rhode-Island and Providence Plantations one, Connecticut five, New-York six, New Jersey four, Pennsylvania eight, Delaware one, Maryland six, Virginia ten, North Carolina five, South Carolina five, and Georgia three.

4: When vacancies happen in the Representation from any State, the Executive Authority thereof shall issue Writs of Election to fill such Vacancies.

5: The House of Representatives shall chuse their Speaker and other Officers; and shall have the sole Power of Impeachment.

Section 3

1: The Senate of the United States shall be composed of two Senators from each State, chosen by the Legislature thereof, for six Years; and each Senator shall have one Vote.

2: Immediately after they shall be assembled in Consequence of the first Election, they shall be divided as equally as may be into three Classes. The Seats of the Senators of the first Class shall be vacated at the Expiration of the second Year, of the second Class at the Expiration of the fourth Year, and of the third Class at the Expiration of the sixth Year, so that one third may be chosen every second Year; and if Vacancies happen by Resignation, or otherwise, during the Recess of the Legislature of any State, the Executive thereof may make temporary Appointments until the next Meeting of the Legislature, which shall then fill such Vacancies.

3: No Person shall be a Senator who shall not have attained to the Age of thirty Years, and been nine Years a Citizen of the United States, and who shall not, when elected, be an Inhabitant of that State for which he shall be chosen.

4: The Vice President of the United States shall be President of the Senate, but shall have no Vote, unless they be equally divided.

5: The Senate shall chuse their other Officers, and also a President pro tempore, in the Absence of the Vice President, or when he shall exercise the Office of President of the United States.

6: The Senate shall have the sole Power to try all Impeachments. When sitting for that Purpose, they shall be on Oath or Affirmation. When the President of the United States is tried, the Chief Justice shall preside: And no Person shall be convicted without the Concurrence of two thirds of the Members present.

7: Judgment in Cases of impeachment shall not extend further than to removal from Office, and disqualification to hold and enjoy any Office of honor, Trust or Profit under the United States: but the Party convicted shall nevertheless be liable and subject to

Indictment, Trial, Judgment and Punishment, according to Law.

Section 4

1: The Times, Places and Manner of holding Elections for Senators and Representatives, shall be prescribed in each State by the Legislature thereof; but the Congress may at any time by Law make or alter such Regulations, except as to the Places of chusing Senators.
2: The Congress shall assemble at least once in every Year, and such Meeting shall be on the first Monday in December, unless they shall by Law appoint a different Day.

Section 5

1: Each House shall be the Judge of the Elections, Returns and Qualifications of its own Members, and a Majority of each shall constitute a Quorum to do Business; but a smaller Number may adjourn from day to day, and may be authorized to compel the Attendance of absent Members, in such Manner, and under such Penalties as each House may provide.
2: Each House may determine the Rules of its Proceedings, punish its Members for disorderly Behaviour, and, with the Concurrence of two thirds, expel a Member.
3: Each House shall keep a Journal of its Proceedings, and from time to time publish the same, excepting such Parts as may in their Judgment require Secrecy; and the Yeas and Nays of the Members of either House on any question shall, at the Desire of one fifth of those Present, be entered on the Journal.

4: Neither House, during the Session of Congress, shall, without the Consent of the other, adjourn for more than three days, nor to any other Place than that in which the two Houses shall be sitting.

Section 6

1: The Senators and Representatives shall receive a Compensation for their Services, to be ascertained by Law, and paid out of the Treasury of the United States. They shall in all Cases, except Treason, Felony and Breach of the Peace, be privileged from Arrest during their Attendance at the Session of their respective Houses, and in going to and returning from the same; and for any Speech or Debate in either House, they shall not be questioned in any other Place.
2: No Senator or Representative shall, during the Time for which he was elected, be appointed to any civil Office under the Authority of the United States, which shall have been created, or the Emoluments whereof shall have been encreased during such time; and no Person holding any Office under the United States, shall be a Member of either House during his Continuance in Office.

Section 7

1: All Bills for raising Revenue shall originate in the House of Representatives; but the Senate may propose or concur with Amendments as on other Bills.
2: Every Bill which shall have passed the House of Representatives and the Senate, shall, before it become a Law, be presented to the President of the United States; If he approve he shall sign it, but if not he shall return it, with his Objections to that House in which it shall have originated, who shall enter the Objections at

large on their Journal, and proceed to reconsider it. If after such Reconsideration two thirds of that House shall agree to pass the Bill, it shall be sent, together with the Objections, to the other House, by which it shall likewise be reconsidered, and if approved by two thirds of that House, it shall become a Law. But in all such Cases the Votes of both Houses shall be determined by yeas and Nays, and the Names of the Persons voting for and against the Bill shall be entered on the Journal of each House respectively. If any Bill shall not be returned by the President within ten Days (Sundays excepted) after it shall have been presented to him, the Same shall be a Law, in like Manner as if he had signed it, unless the Congress by their Adjournment prevent its Return, in which Case it shall not be a Law.

3: Every Order, Resolution, or Vote to which the Concurrence of the Senate and House of Representatives may be necessary (except on a question of Adjournment) shall be presented to the President of the United States; and before the Same shall take Effect, shall be approved by him, or being disapproved by him, shall be repassed by two thirds of the Senate and House of Representatives, according to the Rules and Limitations prescribed in the Case of a Bill.

Section 8

1: The Congress shall have Power To lay and collect Taxes, Duties, Imposts and Excises, to pay the Debts and provide for the common Defence and general Welfare of the United States; but all Duties, Imposts and Excises shall be uniform throughout the United States;

2: To borrow Money on the credit of the United States;

3: To regulate Commerce with foreign Nations, and among the several States, and with the Indian Tribes;

4: To establish an uniform Rule of Naturalization, and uniform Laws on the subject of Bankruptcies throughout the United States;

5: To coin Money, regulate the Value thereof, and of foreign Coin, and fix the Standard of Weights and Measures;

6: To provide for the Punishment of counterfeiting the Securities and current Coin of the United States;

7: To establish Post Offices and post Roads;

8: To promote the Progress of Science and useful Arts, by securing for limited Times to Authors and Inventors the exclusive Right to their respective Writings and Discoveries;

9: To constitute Tribunals inferior to the supreme Court;

10: To define and punish Piracies and Felonies committed on the high Seas, and Offences against the Law of Nations;

11: To declare War, grant Letters of Marque and Reprisal, and make Rules concerning Captures on Land and Water;

12: To raise and support Armies, but no Appropriation of Money to that Use shall be for a longer Term than two Years;

13: To provide and maintain a Navy;

14: To make Rules for the Government and Regulation of the land and naval Forces;

15: To provide for calling forth the Militia to execute the Laws of the Union, suppress Insurrections and repel Invasions;

16: To provide for organizing, arming, and disciplining, the Militia, and for governing such Part of them as may be employed in the Service of the United States, reserving to the States respectively, the

Appointment of the Officers, and the Authority of training the Militia according to the discipline prescribed by Congress;

17: To exercise exclusive Legislation in all Cases whatsoever, over such District (not exceeding ten Miles square) as may, by Cession of particular States, and the Acceptance of Congress, become the Seat of the Government of the United States, and to exercise like Authority over all Places purchased by the Consent of the Legislature of the State in which the Same shall be, for the Erection of Forts, Magazines, Arsenals, dock-Yards, and other needful Buildings;— And

18: To make all Laws which shall be necessary and proper for carrying into Execution the foregoing Powers, and all other Powers vested by this Constitution in the Government of the United States, or in any Department or Officer thereof.

Section 9

1: The Migration or Importation of such Persons as any of the States now existing shall think proper to admit, shall not be prohibited by the Congress prior to the Year one thousand eight hundred and eight, but a Tax or duty may be imposed on such Importation, not exceeding ten dollars for each Person.

2: The Privilege of the Writ of Habeas Corpus shall not be suspended, unless when in Cases of Rebellion or Invasion the public Safety may require it.

3: No Bill of Attainder or ex post facto Law shall be passed.

4: No Capitation, or other direct, Tax shall be laid, unless in Proportion to the Census or Enumeration herein before directed to be taken.

5: No Tax or Duty shall be laid on Articles exported from any State.

6: No Preference shall be given by any Regulation of Commerce or Revenue to the Ports of one State over those of another: nor shall Vessels bound to, or from, one State, be obliged to enter, clear, or pay Duties in another.

7: No Money shall be drawn from the Treasury, but in Consequence of Appropriations made by Law; and a regular Statement and Account of the Receipts and Expenditures of all public Money shall be published from time to time.

8: No Title of Nobility shall be granted by the United States: And no Person holding any Office of Profit or Trust under them, shall, without the Consent of the Congress, accept of any present, Emolument, Office, or Title, of any kind whatever, from any King, Prince, or foreign State.

Section 10

1: No State shall enter into any Treaty, Alliance, or Confederation; grant Letters of Marque and Reprisal; coin Money; emit Bills of Credit; make any Thing but gold and silver Coin a Tender in Payment of Debts; pass any Bill of Attainder, ex post facto Law, or Law impairing the Obligation of Contracts, or grant any Title of Nobility.

2: No State shall, without the Consent of the Congress, lay any Imposts or Duties on Imports or Exports, except what may be absolutely necessary for executing it's inspection Laws: and the net Produce of all Duties and Imposts, laid by any State on Imports or Exports, shall be for the Use of the Treasury of the United States; and all such Laws shall be subject to the Revision and Controul of the Congress.

3: No State shall, without the Consent of Congress, lay any Duty of Tonnage, keep Troops, or Ships of War in time of Peace, enter into any Agreement or Compact with another State, or with a foreign Power, or engage in War, unless actually invaded, or in such imminent Danger as will not admit of delay.

Article II Executive

Section 1

1: The executive Power shall be vested in a President of the United States of America. He shall hold his Office during the Term of four Years, and, together with the Vice President, chosen for the same Term, be elected, as follows
2: Each State shall appoint, in such Manner as the Legislature thereof may direct, a Number of Electors, equal to the whole Number of Senators and Representatives to which the State may be entitled in the Congress: but no Senator or Representative, or Person holding an Office of Trust or Profit under the United States, shall be appointed an Elector.
3: The Electors shall meet in their respective States, and vote by Ballot for two Persons, of whom one at least shall not be an Inhabitant of the same State with themselves. And they shall make a List of all the Persons voted for, and of the Number of Votes for each; which List they shall sign and certify, and transmit sealed to the Seat of the Government of the United States, directed to the President of the Senate. The President of the Senate shall, in the Presence of the Senate and House of Representatives, open all the Certificates, and the Votes shall then be counted. The Person having the greatest Number of Votes shall be the President, if such Number be a Majority of the whole Number of Electors appointed; and if there be more than one who have such Majority, and have an

equal Number of Votes, then the House of Representatives shall immediately chuse by Ballot one of them for President; and if no Person have a Majority, then from the five highest on the List the said House shall in like Manner chuse the President. But in chusing the President, the Votes shall be taken by States, the Representation from each State having one Vote; A quorum for this Purpose shall consist of a Member or Members from two thirds of the States, and a Majority of all the States shall be necessary to a Choice. In every Case, after the Choice of the President, the Person having the greatest Number of Votes of the Electors shall be the Vice President. But if there should remain two or more who have equal Votes, the Senate shall chuse from them by Ballot the Vice President.

4: The Congress may determine the Time of chusing the Electors, and the Day on which they shall give their Votes; which Day shall be the same throughout the United States.

5: No Person except a natural born Citizen, or a Citizen of the United States, at the time of the Adoption of this Constitution, shall be eligible to the Office of President; neither shall any Person be eligible to that Office who shall not have attained to the Age of thirty five Years, and been fourteen Years a Resident within the United States.

6: In Case of the Removal of the President from Office, or of his Death, Resignation, or Inability to discharge the Powers and Duties of the said Office, the Same shall devolve on the Vice President, and the Congress may by Law provide for the Case of Removal, Death, Resignation or Inability, both of the President and Vice President, declaring what Officer shall then act as President, and such Officer shall act accordingly, until the Disability be removed, or a President shall be elected.

7: The President shall, at stated Times, receive for his Services, a Compensation, which shall neither be encreased nor diminished during the Period for which he shall have been elected, and he shall not receive within that Period any other Emolument from the United States, or any of them.

8: Before he enter on the Execution of his Office, he shall take the following Oath or Affirmation:—"I do solemnly swear (or affirm) that I will faithfully execute the Office of President of the United States, and will to the best of my Ability, preserve, protect and defend the Constitution of the United States."

Section 2

1: The President shall be Commander in Chief of the Army and Navy of the United States, and of the Militia of the several States, when called into the actual Service of the United States; he may require the Opinion, in writing, of the principal Officer in each of the executive Departments, upon any Subject relating to the Duties of their respective Offices, and he shall have Power to grant Reprieves and Pardons for Offences against the United States, except in Cases of Impeachment.

2: He shall have Power, by and with the Advice and Consent of the Senate, to make Treaties, provided two thirds of the Senators present concur; and he shall nominate, and by and with the Advice and Consent of the Senate, shall appoint Ambassadors, other public Ministers and Consuls, Judges of the supreme Court, and all other Officers of the United States, whose Appointments are not herein otherwise provided for, and which shall be established by Law: but the

Congress may by Law vest the Appointment of such inferior Officers, as they think proper, in the President alone, in the Courts of Law, or in the Heads of Departments.

3: The President shall have Power to fill up all Vacancies that may happen during the Recess of the Senate, by granting Commissions which shall expire at the End of their next Session.

Section 3

He shall from time to time give to the Congress Information of the State of the Union, and recommend to their Consideration such Measures as he shall judge necessary and expedient; he may, on extraordinary Occasions, convene both Houses, or either of them, and in Case of Disagreement between them, with Respect to the Time of Adjournment, he may adjourn them to such Time as he shall think proper; he shall receive Ambassadors and other public Ministers; he shall take Care that the Laws be faithfully executed, and shall Commission all the Officers of the United States.

Section 4

The President, Vice President and all civil Officers of the United States, shall be removed from Office on Impeachment for, and Conviction of, Treason, Bribery, or other high Crimes and Misdemeanors.

Article III Judicial

Section 1

The judicial Power of the United States, shall be vested in one supreme Court, and in such inferior Courts as the Congress may from time to time ordain and establish. The Judges, both of the supreme and inferior Courts, shall hold their Offices during good Behaviour, and shall, at stated Times, receive for their Services, a Compensation, which shall not be diminished during their Continuance in Office.

Section 2

1: The judicial Power shall extend to all Cases, in Law and Equity, arising under this Constitution, the Laws of the United States, and Treaties made, or which shall be made, under their Authority;—to all Cases affecting Ambassadors, other public Ministers and Consuls;—to all Cases of admiralty and maritime Jurisdiction;—to Controversies to which the United States shall be a Party;—to Controversies between two or more States;—between a State and Citizens of another State; between Citizens of different States, between Citizens of the same State claiming Lands under Grants of different States, and between a State, or the Citizens thereof, and foreign States, Citizens or Subjects.
2: In all Cases affecting Ambassadors, other public Ministers and Consuls, and those in which a State shall be Party, the supreme Court shall have original Jurisdiction. In all the other Cases before mentioned, the supreme Court shall have appellate Jurisdiction, both as to Law and Fact, with such Exceptions, and under such Regulations as the Congress shall make.
3: The Trial of all Crimes, except in Cases of Impeachment, shall be by Jury; and such Trial shall be held in the State where the said Crimes shall have been committed; but when not committed within any State,

the Trial shall be at such Place or Places as the Congress may by Law have directed.

Section 3

1: Treason against the United States, shall consist only in levying War against them, or in adhering to their Enemies, giving them Aid and Comfort. No Person shall be convicted of Treason unless on the Testimony of two Witnesses to the same overt Act, or on Confession in open Court.
2: The Congress shall have Power to declare the Punishment of Treason, but no Attainder of Treason shall work Corruption of Blood, or Forfeiture except during the Life of the Person attainted.

Article IV States' Relations

Section 1

Full Faith and Credit shall be given in each State to the public Acts, Records, and judicial Proceedings of every other State. And the Congress may by general Laws prescribe the Manner in which such Acts, Records and Proceedings shall be proved, and the Effect thereof.

Section 2

1: The Citizens of each State shall be entitled to all Privileges and Immunities of Citizens in the several States.
2: A Person charged in any State with Treason, Felony, or other Crime, who shall flee from Justice, and be found in another State, shall on Demand of the executive Authority of the State from which he fled, be

delivered up, to be removed to the State having Jurisdiction of the Crime.

3: No Person held to Service or Labour in one State, under the Laws thereof, escaping into another, shall, in Consequence of any Law or Regulation therein, be discharged from such Service or Labour, but shall be delivered up on Claim of the Party to whom such Service or Labour may be due.

Section 3

1: New States may be admitted by the Congress into this Union; but no new State shall be formed or erected within the Jurisdiction of any other State; nor any State be formed by the Junction of two or more States, or Parts of States, without the Consent of the Legislatures of the States concerned as well as of the Congress.

2: The Congress shall have Power to dispose of and make all needful Rules and Regulations respecting the Territory or other Property belonging to the United States; and nothing in this Constitution shall be so construed as to Prejudice any Claims of the United States, or of any particular State.

Section 4

The United States shall guarantee to every State in this Union a Republican Form of Government, and shall protect each of them against Invasion; and on Application of the Legislature, or of the Executive (when the Legislature cannot be convened) against domestic Violence.

Article V Mode of Amendment

The Congress, whenever two thirds of both Houses shall deem it necessary, shall propose Amendments to this Constitution, or, on the Application of the Legislatures of two thirds of the several States, shall call a Convention for proposing Amendments, which, in either Case, shall be valid to all Intents and Purposes, as Part of this Constitution, when ratified by the Legislatures of three fourths of the several States, or by Conventions in three fourths thereof, as the one or the other Mode of Ratification may be proposed by the Congress; Provided that no Amendment which may be made prior to the Year One thousand eight hundred and eight shall in any Manner affect the first and fourth Clauses in the Ninth Section of the first Article; and that no State, without its Consent, shall be deprived of its equal Suffrage in the Senate.

Article VI Prior Debts, National Supremacy, Oaths of Office

1: All Debts contracted and Engagements entered into, before the Adoption of this Constitution, shall be as valid against the United States under this Constitution, as under the Confederation.
2: This Constitution, and the Laws of the United States which shall be made in Pursuance thereof; and all Treaties made, or which shall be made, under the Authority of the United States, shall be the supreme Law of the Land; and the Judges in every State shall be bound thereby, any Thing in the Constitution or Laws of any State to the Contrary notwithstanding.
3: The Senators and Representatives before mentioned, and the Members of the several State Legislatures, and all executive and judicial Officers, both of the United States and of the several States, shall be bound by Oath or Affirmation, to support this Constitution; but no

religious Test shall ever be required as a Qualification to any Office or public Trust under the United States.

Article VII Ratification

The Ratification of the Conventions of nine States, shall be sufficient for the Establishment of this Constitution between the States so ratifying the Same.

Amendments

Amendment 1 - Freedom of expression and religion

Congress shall make no law respecting an establishment of religion, or prohibiting the free exercise thereof; or abridging the freedom of speech, or of the press; or the right of the people peaceably to assemble, and to petition the Government for a redress of grievances.

Amendment 2 - Bearing Arms

A well regulated Militia, being necessary to the security of a free State, the right of the people to keep and bear Arms, shall not be infringed.

Amendment 3 - Quartering Soldiers

No Soldier shall, in time of peace be quartered in any house, without the consent of the Owner, nor in time of war, but in a manner to be prescribed by law.

Amendment 4 - Search and Seizure

The right of the people to be secure in their persons, houses, papers, and effects, against unreasonable searches and seizures, shall not be violated, and no Warrants shall issue, but upon probable cause, supported by Oath or affirmation, and particularly describing the place to be searched, and the persons or things to be seized.

Amendment 5 - Rights of Persons

No person shall be held to answer for a capital, or otherwise infamous crime, unless on a presentment or indictment of a Grand Jury, except in cases arising in the land or naval forces, or in the Militia, when in actual service in time of War or public danger; nor shall any person be subject for the same offence to be twice put in jeopardy of life or limb; nor shall be compelled in any criminal case to be a witness against himself, nor be deprived of life, liberty, or property, without due process of law; nor shall private property be taken for public use, without just compensation.

Amendment 6 - Rights of Accused in Criminal Prosecutions

In all criminal prosecutions, the accused shall enjoy the right to a speedy and public trial, by an impartial jury of the State and district wherein the crime shall have been committed, which district shall have been previously ascertained by law, and to be informed of the nature and cause of the accusation; to be confronted with the witnesses against him; to have compulsory process for obtaining witnesses in his favor, and to have the Assistance of Counsel for his defence.

Amendment 7 - Civil Trials

In Suits at common law, where the value in controversy shall exceed twenty dollars, the right of trial by jury shall be preserved, and no fact tried by a jury, shall be otherwise re-examined in any Court of the United States, than according to the rules of the common law.

Amendment 8 - Further Guarantees in Criminal Cases

Excessive bail shall not be required, nor excessive fines imposed, nor cruel and unusual punishments inflicted.

Amendment 9 - Unenumerated Rights

The enumeration in the Constitution of certain rights, shall not be construed to deny or disparage others retained by the people.

Amendment 10 - Reserved Powers

The powers not delegated to the United States by the Constitution, nor prohibited by it to the States, are reserved to the States respectively, or to the people.

Amendment 11 - Suits Against States

The Judicial power of the United States shall not be construed to extend to any suit in law or equity, commenced or prosecuted against one of the United States by Citizens of another State, or by Citizens or Subjects of any Foreign State.

Amendment 12 - Election of President

The Electors shall meet in their respective states, and vote by ballot for President and Vice-President, one of whom, at least, shall not be an inhabitant of the same state with themselves; they shall name in their ballots the person voted for as President, and in distinct ballots the person voted for as Vice-President, and they shall make distinct lists of all persons voted for as President, and of all persons voted for as Vice-President, and of the number of votes for each, which lists they shall sign and certify, and transmit sealed to the seat of the government of the United States, directed to the President of the Senate;—The President of the Senate shall, in the presence of the Senate and House of Representatives, open all the certificates and the votes shall then be counted;—The person having the greatest number of votes for President, shall be the President, if such number be a majority of the whole number of Electors appointed; and if no person have such majority, then from the persons having the highest numbers not exceeding three on the list of those voted for as President, the House of Representatives shall choose immediately, by ballot, the President. But in choosing the President, the votes shall be taken by states, the representation from each state having one vote; a quorum for this purpose shall consist of a member or members from two-thirds of the states, and a majority of all the states shall be necessary to a choice. And if the House of Representatives shall not choose a President whenever the right of choice shall devolve upon them, before the fourth day of March next following, then the Vice-President shall act as President, as in the case of the death or other constitutional disability of the President. The person having the greatest number of votes as Vice-President, shall be the Vice-President, if such number be a majority of the whole number of Electors appointed, and if no person have a majority, then from the two highest numbers on the list, the Senate shall choose the Vice-President; a quorum for the purpose shall consist of two-thirds of the whole number of Senators, and a majority of the whole number shall be necessary to a choice. But no person constitutionally ineligible to the office of President shall be eligible to that of Vice-President of the United States.

Amendment 13 - Slavery and Involuntary Servitude

Neither slavery nor involuntary servitude, except as a punishment for crime whereof the party shall have been duly convicted, shall exist within the United States, or any place subject to their jurisdiction.
Congress shall have power to enforce this article by appropriate legislation.

Amendment 14 - Rights Guaranteed: Privileges and Immunities of Citizenship, Due Process, and Equal Protection

1: All persons born or naturalized in the United States, and subject to the jurisdiction thereof, are citizens of the United States and of the State wherein they reside. No State shall make or enforce any law which shall abridge the privileges or immunities of citizens of the United States; nor shall any State deprive any person of life, liberty, or property, without due process of law; nor deny to any person within its jurisdiction the equal protection of the laws.
2: Representatives shall be apportioned among the several States according to their respective numbers, counting the whole number of persons in each State, excluding Indians not taxed. But when the right to vote

at any election for the choice of electors for President and Vice President of the United States, Representatives in Congress, the Executive and Judicial officers of a State, or the members of the Legislature thereof, is denied to any of the male inhabitants of such State, being twenty-one years of age, and citizens of the United States, or in any way abridged, except for participation in rebellion, or other crime, the basis of representation therein shall be reduced in the proportion which the number of such male citizens shall bear to the whole number of male citizens twenty-one years of age in such State.

3: No person shall be a Senator or Representative in Congress, or elector of President and Vice President, or hold any office, civil or military, under the United States, or under any State, who, having previously taken an oath, as a member of Congress, or as an officer of the United States, or as a member of any State legislature, or as an executive or judicial officer of any State, to support the Constitution of the United States, shall have engaged in insurrection or rebellion against the same, or given aid or comfort to the enemies thereof. But Congress may by a vote of two-thirds of each House, remove such disability.

4: The validity of the public debt of the United States, authorized by law, including debts incurred for payment of pensions and bounties for services in suppressing insurrection or rebellion, shall not be questioned. But neither the United States nor any State shall assume or pay any debt or obligation incurred in aid of insurrection or rebellion against the United States, or any claim for the loss or emancipation of any slave; but all such debts, obligations and claims shall be held illegal and void.

5: The Congress shall have power to enforce, by appropriate legislation, the provisions of this article.

Amendment 15 - Rights of Citizens to Vote

The right of citizens of the United States to vote shall not be denied or abridged by the United States or by any State on account of race, color, or previous condition of servitude.
The Congress shall have power to enforce this article by appropriate legislation.

Amendment 16 - Income Tax

The Congress shall have power to lay and collect taxes on incomes, from whatever source derived, without apportionment among the several States, and without regard to any census or enumeration.

Amendment 17 - Popular Election of Senators

1: The Senate of the United States shall be composed of two Senators from each State, elected by the people thereof, for six years; and each Senator shall have one vote. The electors in each State shall have the qualifications requisite for electors of the most numerous branch of the State legislatures.
2: When vacancies happen in the representation of any State in the Senate, the executive authority of such State shall issue writs of election to fill such vacancies: Provided, That the legislature of any State may empower the executive thereof to make temporary appointments until the people fill the vacancies by election as the legislature may direct.
3: This amendment shall not be so construed as to affect the election or term of any Senator chosen before it becomes valid as part of the Constitution.

Amendment 18 - Prohibition of Intoxicating Liquors

1: After one year from the ratification of this article the manufacture, sale, or transportation of intoxicating liquors within, the importation thereof into, or the exportation thereof from the United States and all territory subject to the jurisdiction thereof for beverage purposes is hereby prohibited.
2: The Congress and the several States shall have concurrent power to enforce this article by appropriate legislation.
3: This article shall be inoperative unless it shall have been ratified as an amendment to the Constitution by the legislatures of the several States, as provided in the Constitution, within seven years from the date of the submission hereof to the States by the Congress.

Amendment 19 - Women's Suffrage Rights

The right of citizens of the United States to vote shall not be denied or abridged by the United States or by any State on account of sex.
Congress shall have power to enforce this article by appropriate legislation.

Amendment 20 - Terms of President, Vice President, Members of Congress: Presidential Vacancy

1: The terms of the President and Vice President shall end at noon on the 20th day of January, and the terms of Senators and Representatives at noon on the 3d day of January, of the years in which such terms would have ended if this article had not been ratified; and the terms of their successors shall then begin.
2: The Congress shall assemble at least once in every year, and such meeting shall begin at noon on the 3d

day of January, unless they shall by law appoint a different day.

3: If, at the time fixed for the beginning of the term of the President, the President elect shall have died, the Vice President elect shall become President. If a President shall not have been chosen before the time fixed for the beginning of his term, or if the President elect shall have failed to qualify, then the Vice President elect shall act as President until a President shall have qualified; and the Congress may by law provide for the case wherein neither a President elect nor a Vice President elect shall have qualified, declaring who shall then act as President, or the manner in which one who is to act shall be selected, and such person shall act accordingly until a President or Vice President shall have qualified.

4: The Congress may by law provide for the case of the death of any of the persons from whom the House of Representatives may choose a President whenever the right of choice shall have devolved upon them, and for the case of the death of any of the persons from whom the Senate may choose a Vice President whenever the right of choice shall have devolved upon them.

5: Sections 1 and 2 shall take effect on the 15th day of October following the ratification of this article.

6: This article shall be inoperative unless it shall have been ratified as an amendment to the Constitution by the legislatures of three-fourths of the several States within seven years from the date of its submission.

Amendment 21 - Repeal of Eighteenth Amendment

1: The eighteenth article of amendment to the Constitution of the United States is hereby repealed.

2: The transportation or importation into any State, Territory, or possession of the United States for delivery or use therein of intoxicating liquors, in violation of the laws thereof, is hereby prohibited.

3: This article shall be inoperative unless it shall have been ratified as an amendment to the Constitution by conventions in the several States, as provided in the Constitution, within seven years from the date of the submission hereof to the States by the Congress.

Amendment 22 - Presidential Tenure

1: No person shall be elected to the office of the President more than twice, and no person who has held the office of President, or acted as President, for more than two years of a term to which some other person was elected President shall be elected to the office of the President more than once. But this article shall not apply to any person holding the office of President when this article was proposed by the Congress, and shall not prevent any person who may be holding the office of President, or acting as President, during the term within which this article becomes operative from holding the office of President or acting as President during the remainder of such term.

2: This article shall be inoperative unless it shall have been ratified as an amendment to the Constitution by the legislatures of three-fourths of the several states within seven years from the date of its submission to the states by the Congress.

Amendment 23 - Presidential Electors for the District of Columbia

1: The District constituting the seat of government of the United States shall appoint in such manner as the Congress may direct: A number of electors of President and Vice President equal to the whole

number of Senators and Representatives in Congress to which the District would be entitled if it were a state, but in no event more than the least populous state; they shall be in addition to those appointed by the states, but they shall be considered, for the purposes of the election of President and Vice President, to be electors appointed by a state; and they shall meet in the District and perform such duties as provided by the twelfth article of amendment.
2: The Congress shall have power to enforce this article by appropriate legislation.

Amendment 24 - Abolition of the Poll Tax Qualification in Federal Elections

1. The right of citizens of the United States to vote in any primary or other election for President or Vice President, for electors for President or Vice President, or for Senator or Representative in Congress, shall not be denied or abridged by the United States or any state by reason of failure to pay any poll tax or other tax.
2. The Congress shall have power to enforce this article by appropriate legislation.

Amendment 25 - Presidential Vacancy, Disability, and Inability

1: In case of the removal of the President from office or of his death or resignation, the Vice President shall become President.
2: Whenever there is a vacancy in the office of the Vice President, the President shall nominate a Vice President who shall take office upon confirmation by a majority vote of both Houses of Congress.
3: Whenever the President transmits to the President pro tempore of the Senate and the Speaker of the

House of Representatives his written declaration that he is unable to discharge the powers and duties of his office, and until he transmits to them a written declaration to the contrary, such powers and duties shall be discharged by the Vice President as Acting President.

4: Whenever the Vice President and a majority of either the principal officers of the executive departments or of such other body as Congress may by law provide, transmit to the President pro tempore of the Senate and the Speaker of the House of Representatives their written declaration that the President is unable to discharge the powers and duties of his office, the Vice President shall immediately assume the powers and duties of the office as Acting President.

Thereafter, when the President transmits to the President pro tempore of the Senate and the Speaker of the House of Representatives his written declaration that no inability exists, he shall resume the powers and duties of his office unless the Vice President and a majority of either the principal officers of the executive department or of such other body as Congress may by law provide, transmit within four days to the President pro tempore of the Senate and the Speaker of the House of Representatives their written declaration that the President is unable to discharge the powers and duties of his office. Thereupon Congress shall decide the issue, assembling within forty-eight hours for that purpose if not in session. If the Congress, within twenty-one days after receipt of the latter written declaration, or, if Congress is not in session, within twenty-one days after Congress is required to assemble, determines by two-thirds vote of both Houses that the President is unable to discharge the powers and duties of his office, the Vice President shall continue to discharge the same as Acting President; otherwise, the President shall resume the powers and duties of his office.

Amendment 26 - Reduction of Voting Age Qualification

1: The right of citizens of the United States, who are 18 years of age or older, to vote, shall not be denied or abridged by the United States or any state on account of age.
2: The Congress shall have the power to enforce this article by appropriate legislation.

Amendment 27 - Congressional Pay Limitation

No law varying the compensation for the services of the Senators and Representatives shall take effect until an election of Representatives shall have intervened.

ESSAYS ON GOVERNMENT

These writings first appeared on a coastal California newspaper website, often in response to events of the time. The first essay, on privacy issues, was written in the wake of the 2013 Snowden revelations about NSA data gathering. Three essays on money in politics followed the Supreme Court's 2010 Citizens United decision and aftermath. The five pieces on health care reform spanned the period from the 2010 signing into law of the Affordable Care Act, through its consideration before the Supreme Court in 2012.

July 12, 2013
THE FOURTH AMENDMENT V. THE SURVEILLANCE STATE: A SYNOPSIS AND A SOLUTION

What can the government lawfully learn about us, without our consent or a court warrant? That is the question to be explored below. The answer, constitutionally, is largely confined to the Fourth Amendment:

"The right of the people to be secure in their persons, houses, papers, and effects, against unreasonable searches and seizures, shall not be violated, and no Warrants shall issue, but upon probable cause, supported by Oath or affirmation, and particularly describing the place to be searched, and the persons or things to be seized."

JUDICIAL INTERPRETATION WITHOUT A COMPASS

The original language is clear, but its judicial interpretation has a stumbling history. It wasn't until 1914 – more than 120 years later – that the Supreme Court affirmed the amendment's plain intent that a warrantless search of a home is unconstitutional, while adding as a deterrent that evidence thus obtained is inadmissible. It was 1961 before Fourth Amendment strictures were applied to state and local government, and 1967 before warrantless telephone wiretaps were outlawed. In 1976, reversing course, the Supreme Court decided that government could examine our bank records without warrant; in 1979, that the government could track our telephone use without warrant. Since then, Fourth Amendment rulings have (more times than not) eroded privacy protections, whether about searches on the street, from the air, using remote devices, in a car, upon arrest, detention, even a traffic violation. Now in the post-9/11 era, given the Patriot Act and a surveillance state that has understandably swelled in response to terrorism, the judiciary continues to stumble along. Why? Because it lacks an overarching constitutional interpretative principle – a legal compass – to guide its Fourth Amendment decisions.

How can we know this? Because the pair of Fourth Amendment principles most often employed as interpretative precedents are either misapplied (in the case of #1 below), or simply wrong (#2):

1. Government needs a warrant to search in a context where the public has a "reasonable expectation of privacy."

2. When communications between parties use a third-party intermediary or facilitator (e.g., a phone company, internet provider, bank), the information the third-party is given to know is not private; therefore the government does not need a warrant to search it. This is commonly referred to as the "third party doctrine."

THE ESSENCE OF PRIVACY, AND THE MEANING OF 'SEARCH'

Before we examine these two legal principles, the notion of privacy (which pervades the discussion) should be clarified. Take, for example, the way we use the word in the expression "private property." When we say "private property" we primarily mean (among other things) a space from which others can be physically excluded. That is the essence of privacy: the ability to exclude others from a physical area like a piece of property, or to exclude others from control over or knowledge of aspects of one's own life. The exclusion of others from aspects of one's life can take many forms. It may mean simply to be left alone, unmolested; or the ability to make decisions for oneself (abortion, suicide); or in the case of searches (our subject here), the ability to keep information about oneself secret from others. That is what we consider our private realm: to restrict others from entering our private space, or making decisions for us and dictating our actions, or even acquiring information about us we wish to keep to ourselves.

Also on the subject of words and concepts essential to this discussion, clarity should be brought to the often tortured legal meaning given to the notion of a 'search.' In common parlance, whenever we search, we are looking for something, or more generally, seeking to acquire information. It doesn't matter how the search is conducted. It may be done in any manner, with any device, at a distance or not. It can be done in a laboratory, using the internet, or with a telescope, by looking in a desk, or over a fence, or digging in the ground. Whenever and however we are looking for something (perhaps we know not what), we are searching for and seeking out information.

Judicial interpretation of the Fourth Amendment has unnecessarily confused the issue by conflating the notion of a search with that of a physical invasion. So in some key legal decisions, the outcome has turned on whether an investigation was done remotely, at a distance, without physically entering or invading a "constitutionally protected area," in which case it has not been considered a search, and thus not subject to Fourth Amendment warrant strictures. Using this ruse, a bug placed in one's living room would be considered a search, but a remote high-tech listening device used at a distance might not be. This is a legal sleight-of-hand, and should be abandoned in favor of the commonly understood meaning of a search: any effort intended to look for something.

1. "A REASONABLE EXPECTATION OF PRIVACY"

In Katz v. United States (1967), a man making calls from a phone booth, involving betting transactions, was taped without warrant by a bug attached to the outside of the booth. The evidence thus acquired was thrown out at the Supreme Court, where it was reasoned that the man, being in a phone booth, had a reasonable expectation of privacy. This was a landmark decision, because he wasn't in his home, just in a space that was obviously designed for a modicum of privacy.

The legal reasoning overshot its target however, because it depended in part on discerning the man's actual expectations of privacy. That can't be the deciding factor, because another person in exactly the same position, behaving in exactly the same way, only with possibly a different set of expectations, shouldn't receive an opposite legal outcome. Besides, who can really divine what one person's expectations actually were at the moment of surveillance? So long as the person took the elementary precautions to ensure privacy (closed the booth door, didn't shout into the mouthpiece or otherwise draw undo public attention to his conversation), the assumption is that privacy was expected.

The kernel of legal reasoning that had staying power wasn't the individual's expectations; rather it was the justices' recognition that society has a reasonable expectation of privacy when entering a phone booth, or performing some other activities. Like a bathroom stall with a door, a phone booth is recognized by society as private by design.

Here we arrive at the crucial question about this legal yardstick: is it society's expectation that some situation or context is in fact private, or that it should be private? In other words, is the legal yardstick – society's reasonable expectation of privacy – factual ("it is private") or normative ("it should be private")?

FACTUAL EXPECTATIONS OF PRIVACY: A FOURTH AMENDMENT TRAPDOOR

Simply put, it can't be factual, because we are rapidly entering a technological age where anything and everything can conceivably be surveilled. Private conversations and physical activity anywhere, including inside homes, can already be remotely and minutely searched and recorded. Our unexpressed thoughts are the only things in our lives that we can factually expect to be truly private, and for all we know the clock may be ticking down on that final frontier as well. Bottom line: any legal principle that hangs on what society can actually, factually, expect to be private, given the rapid advance of surveillance technology, would push the Fourth Amendment through a trapdoor. Privacy rights cannot be inversely proportional to the march of technology, without shriveling to nothing.

NORMATIVE EXPECTATIONS OF PRIVACY: A FOURTH AMENDMENT PRINCIPLE

If the answer to the question above is that society has a set of reasonable expectations of what should be private, and that those expectations should provide the yardstick for adjudicating Fourth Amendment issues, what if we (society) disagree on what should be private? What if there is no general consensus on a particular privacy issue?

If there is no societal consensus on a privacy issue, then on that issue, society has no reasonable expectation of privacy. We do not need an obviously unattainable unanimity, but an overwhelming consensus, in order to determine that society has a reasonable expectation of privacy concerning an activity or context.

There are many examples of privacy consensus across society. We agree that what we do in our homes should be private, if we pull our shades; that our conversations should be private, if conducted out of others' earshot; that our dealings with our doctors, or shrinks, or lawyers, should be confidential; that neighbors should not look at or open our mail; that our computers and electronic devices should not be hacked; that doors on private bathrooms, and public bathroom stalls, should be lockable; and on and on.

Indeed, a working definition of "reasonable" expectations is that society has a consensus; if there is no consensus, the expectation is almost by legal definition not reasonable. Almost, but not quite, because if some of us can convince most of us that something should be considered private, and thereby change people's minds and form a new consensus, a new "reasonable expectation of privacy" is thereby created, and the privacy realm is expanded.

Our society's consensus on privacy issues has inevitably evolved over time. In fact, contrary to some recent punditry, our society has been rapidly expanding – not shrinking – its privacy-realm consensus over the last decades, evolving toward a less invasive, more private society. Routine prying questions from yesteryear, when seeking a job or housing or medical assistance or an education or social benefits, are now piles of illegal relics. Over the same decades we have even had a flock of fairly controversial legal innovations, such as exclusionary rules of evidence, or Miranda rights, or contraceptive and abortion rights, that arguably did not reflect a societal consensus, but that nevertheless expanded the privacy realm for individuals in a variety of directions. Privacy rights, consensus or no, like them or not, have been expanding throughout our history.

A ONE-STANDARD "PRIVACY PRINCIPLE" FOR BOTH THE PUBLIC AND GOVERNMENT

As a society, we have an elaborate (if often unspoken) consensus on reasonable expectations of privacy between ourselves. We do not have a separate set of reasonable expectations of privacy with respect to the government. As we do not consider it appropriate for the neighbor to read our mail, neither do we consider it appropriate for the government. We do not consider it appropriate for either our neighbor or our government to peer in our windows, or over a bathroom stall wall, or hack our computers, or listen in on our phone calls. Unless convinced otherwise, we simply do not operate – nor should we – with two distinct sets of expectations about what we should be able to keep private from the public on the one hand, and from the government on the other. The privacy standards that we maintain between ourselves, as members of society, are exactly the privacy standards that should be maintained between ourselves and our government, absent a court warrant based on evidence of criminal activity. There is no other standard, and should not be, because government, like the public, is a collection or organization of persons. This one-standard privacy principle can be stated in general form:

"Whatever the public cannot lawfully learn about someone without his or her permission, the government should not be able to learn without a court warrant."

By using society's consensus on reasonable expectations of privacy, applied as one unified standard for both the public and government, the courts will have a guiding principle that we are all familiar with, and automatically use every day to conduct our lives within society, to decide Fourth Amendment issues. Most important, it would destroy the pernicious "third party doctrine" that is currently used to legally condone an ever-expanding surveillance state.

2. THE THIRD PARTY DOCTRINE: THE MOTHER OF ALL PRIVACY SLIPPERY SLOPES

The third party doctrine – that the information provided by private communicants to a third-party intermediary is not itself private – is not a common sense doctrine, in that it is not intuitively obvious, nor based squarely on our reasonable expectations of privacy, and so must be motivated by looking at its modern impetus in two Supreme Court cases from the 1970s.

PRIVACY OF BANK RECORDS

The first, United States v. Miller (1976), involved the issue of whether the government may lawfully examine one's bank records without a warrant. A 5-4 majority upheld that ability, with the following reasoning:

"The depositor takes the risk, in revealing his affairs to another, that the information will be conveyed by that person to the Government. This Court has held repeatedly that the Fourth Amendment does not prohibit the obtaining of information revealed to a third party and conveyed by him to Government authorities, even if the information is revealed on the assumption that it will be used only for a limited purpose and the confidence placed in the third party will not be betrayed."

This statement is erroneous in a number of ways. Its first sentence is based on reasoning from a Jimmy Hoffa case, where Hoffa unsuccessfully tried to have testimony from an undercover FBI informant excluded from his trial. Apart from tellingly analogizing the behavior of an FBI mole to one's bank, it states without qualification that any information revealed to a second party ('another,' even a doctor, shrink, or lawyer) can be lawfully revealed to the government, a nightmare scenario clearly to be avoided. The second sentence then slides from a discussion of a second party to that of a third party, which is presumably the position a bank assumes with respect to a depositor.

A bank is actually only a second party to a depositor, holding his or her money for safekeeping. In taking one's money from underneath the mattress into the bank to deposit, there is no third party. The bank becomes a third party if it is used to cash a check, or pay by check, or in our time, to also pay bills online. In other words, a bank can be solely a second party, if all one has is a savings account (or CDs, etc.). So the third party doctrine does not necessarily apply, while the second party justification is based on an FBI mole analogy, where the target is suspected of crime. Yet the Supreme Court ruled that the government may examine our bank records without a warrant, and without suspicion of a crime.

The minority dissent made a prescient warning:

"Development of photocopying machines, electronic computers and other sophisticated instruments have accelerated the ability of government to intrude into areas which a person normally chooses to exclude from prying eyes and inquisitive minds. Consequently, judicial interpretations of the constitutional protection of individual privacy must keep pace with the perils created by these new devices."

PRIVACY OF COMMUNICATIONS 'METADATA'

The Supreme Court decision most relevant to the current discussion of state surveillance is Smith v. Maryland (1979), which upheld the government's ability to gather information about one's phone calls, other than the words themselves, without warrant. In today's discussion, the words are referred to as the "content" of the call, while everything else (the time and length of the call, the telephone numbers involved and to whom they're registered, the communicants' locations during the call, etc.) is known as the "metadata." Current reasoning is that this Supreme Court ruling provides the best constitutional justification for warrantless surveillance of metadata, not only for telephones (land and cell), but also for all internet communications, or indeed any communications using a third-party intermediary. The reasoning is easily analogized to all non-cash financial activity, including credit and debit card transactions, as well as library borrowings, web browsing, satellite and cable television channel surfing and PPV, and USPS and special delivery mail and packages, all of which require third-party intermediaries.

Here is the kernel of the majority's opinion:

"When petitioner voluntarily conveyed numerical information to the phone company and 'exposed' that information to its equipment in the normal course of business, he assumed the risk that the company would reveal the information to the police."

And from a dissenting opinion:

"I think that the numbers dialed from a private telephone - like the conversations that occur during a call - are within the constitutional protection recognized in Katz. It seems clear to me that information obtained by pen register surveillance of a private telephone is information in which the telephone subscriber has a legitimate expectation of privacy." (A pen register was the device of that era used to surveil telephone metadata.)

The dissent correctly points out that collection of telephone metadata violates society's reasonable expectations of privacy, in 1979 as it does now (witness the recent public outcry). But that is not the elephant in the living room.

Look back at the Supreme Court majority opinions cited, where "...the Fourth Amendment does not prohibit the obtaining of information revealed to a third party..." and the public assuming "... the risk that the company would reveal the information to the police." Where's the elephant?

CONTENT AND METADATA ARE ALL THIRD PARTY INFORMATION

When one makes a phone call, or sends an email, or uses a social networking website to communicate with others, the information shared with the third party intermediary is not merely the metadata. It is the content of the message as well. That is the communicant's entire purpose for using the intermediary, to have it convey the message, which naturally cannot be transmitted without the message's actual content. So that the reasoning used above to justify surveillance of metadata, works equally well for surveilling content. Content is no less "exposed" to the third party's "equipment in the normal course of business" than is the metadata. And in the case of written internet communications, it is no less preserved.

There is no way around the fact that when communicants use a third-party intermediary, as we all do many times daily, all of the information – content and metadata – is communicated to and through the third party. And by the language of the controlling Supreme Court decisions cited above, it is all subject to warrantless search. If the third party doctrine were true, and universally and equally applied, all information held by a third party would be subject to warrantless search. Very little of our lives would remain private.

THE THIRD PARTY DOCTRINE V. THE PRIVACY PRINCIPLE

Whenever one uses a bank, credit card company, telephone or internet provider, library, postal or delivery service, doctor, shrink, lawyer, pharmacist, accountant, even a store or restaurant, one has a reasonable expectation that the third party will respect one's privacy, by not revealing the details of one's communications or transactions with other members of the public. These relationships of trust are so universal and implied that we don't think about them. But they're there. Next time you get to the front of the line at the bank, or doctor's office, or pharmacy, or post office, or grocery store, ask the person helping you to tell you some of the juicy details of the last person they served, like why they're seeing the doctor, or what prescriptions they just picked up, or who they just mailed, or their credit card numbers, or even their name. Chances are the next person you'll be speaking to after that performance will be a security guard, and then the police. Our society takes very seriously the almost ubiquitous obligations of confidentiality we assume in our relationships, whether personal or professional, business or pleasure.

In other words, the reasonable expectations of privacy we have developed toward one another are the polar opposite of the third party doctrine, which gives government warrantless and secret access to all information about us held by third parties, information that those parties are expected in normal circumstances to jealously protect from public view. This collision course – between the public's reasonable expectations of privacy and a mistaken legal doctrine blessing an ever-expanding surveillance state – can be avoided by employing the privacy principle stated above:

"Whatever the public cannot lawfully learn about someone without his or her permission, the government should not be able to learn without a court warrant."

May 25, 2012
DO PUBLIC OFFICIALS HAVE FIDUCIARY OBLIGATIONS TO US?

Maybe you think they do, by law. This essay will attempt to disabuse you of that comforting but unfortunately unfounded notion.

Maybe you think they ought to, which is the point I'm going to try to argue here. Because if politicians – both elected and appointed – were considered by civil and criminal law to be fiduciaries, and have basic fiduciary obligations to the public they purportedly serve, we'd have a much cleaner political system. A whole lot of common abuses would be illegalized in one fell swoop.

First we need to define what a fiduciary is. A fiduciary is someone who assumes responsibility for and acts in someone else's interests. Examples of fiduciaries include doctors, lawyers, accountants, real estate salespersons and brokers, financial managers and stockbrokers, corporate and union officers, literary and artistic agents, even parents and pet owners.

I roll out this smorgasbord shortlist to underscore how varied these different fiduciaries are in their respective roles, because different types of fiduciaries have different types of obligations and responsibilities. A doctor's primary fiduciary responsibility to you is to do his or her best to keep you alive and healthy. That is similar to the primary legal obligation a parent or pet owner assumes. A lawyer's primary fiduciary obligation is to represent your legal interests, for example to zealously defend you against criminal charges. Financial managers' primary responsibility is to husband the money you have entrusted to them, and give you honest advice about investing. Honest in the sense that they believe the information and advice to be true, and the recommended course of action is what they would pursue, if they were in your circumstance.

There are many subtleties to fiduciary obligations. Doctors and parents have greater latitude to lie than do lawyers and financial managers. Most fiduciaries become so only upon the agreement of those whose interests they represent. This is not true for those representing the interests of children or pets or adults who lack the capacity to enter into agreements. Some fiduciary obligations are enshrined in criminal law, so that it is a crime to violate them. The rest are civil strictures, so that their violation is a tort against the offended party, subject to civil action.

As you see, fiduciary obligations can be multifarious, and far from cut-and-dry. So let's focus on a type of fiduciary relationship that is a little less ambiguous than others: when someone represents you and your interests in a negotiation. That person is known as your agent, and you are known as the principal. The agent's purpose is to arrive at a contract or agreement that maximizes your interests as you have represented them to your agent. Your interests are in contradistinction to the interests of the party or parties you are negotiating with. Your agent is obligated to represent only your interests, not to attempt to balance the interests of all the parties. If all parties and their agents represent their interests separately, the proper balance should be reflected in the agreement, since presumably all parties enter the agreement voluntarily.

Your agent may be representing you in your effort to come to a transactional agreement with another party to buy or sell something (real estate, a company, patent, etc.), or to enter into a service contract, where you agree to do something, in return for the other party doing something. When lawyers haggle over the terms of a pre-nup, they are agents negotiating the terms of a marriage contract for their respective principals. In all the different contractual negotiations under the sun, there is one thing agents cannot do and still fulfill their fiduciary obligations.

Suppose that you have hired an agent to help sell your family farm. You don't know – you can never know – that the person you've hired is actually representing your interests to the best of their ability. That's why the word 'fiduciary' is from the Latin word for 'trust' (think 'semper fi'), because you are ultimately trusting and having faith that your agent will act in your interests, and only in your interests. Will the agent try to convince you to take a lower price than you should for the farm, so he or she can get a commission and move on? Is your agent actually pals with the buyer or buyer's agent? You probably will never know for certain.

One elementary way that we try to protect against collusion between your agent and the parties you're negotiating with is to create a financial firewall between them and your agent. That is, your agent is prohibited from receiving money from the other parties without your permission. There are two underlying notions behind the prohibition. First, that an agent cannot serve two masters who have competing interests. So it is a necessary condition – a bedrock fiduciary obligation in any negotiation – that an agent of a principal not receive financial benefit from the counterparty. The second underlying legal concept is 'conflict of interest': where someone receives a personal benefit that vitiates an extra-personal responsibility, in this case a fiduciary obligation to a principal. Accordingly, if the agent is receiving money from a competing party, you may assume that the fiduciary obligation to represent only your interests has been violated. Maybe it actually hasn't, but the law considers it prima facie evidence that the agent, through a conflict of interest, has violated his or her fiduciary obligation to negotiate solely on your behalf.

Now let's look at the case of an elected public official, representing a constituency. It certainly fits the general definition of a fiduciary, someone who takes responsibility for and acts in someone else's interests, namely, the public within the jurisdiction of the office. This is reflected in the language we customarily use to describe the relationship: the elected official is our representative, that is, elected to represent our interests. He or she takes an oath of office that may include language implying fiduciary obligation to the public.

Here's where the proof lies, that in fact a public official is not at present held to the most basic fiduciary obligation to the public: in negotiations – say between legislators and a labor union or corporation – the union or corporation is free to give campaign donations and even lobbying gifts to some or all of the legislators with whom they negotiate. In fact, this is customary, almost universal. One would be hard-pressed to find any negotiation that has occurred between any legislature and any union or corporation in which some or most of the legislators did not receive direct financial benefit from the parties they are supposedly in negotiations with, on behalf of the public. If laws prohibit direct contributions, there are plenty of workarounds: super PACs, soft money, flocks of 'individual' donors, etc.

What results, when legislators and other public officials receive financial benefit from parties with whom they are supposedly negotiating on behalf of the public, is a sweetheart contract. Sweetheart contracts are often marked by their long-term lack of viability, where the terms of the contract become increasingly unrealizable over time. The prime examples before us in California are the sweetheart contracts that our state legislature has negotiated with public-sector unions, especially over pensions. It doesn't matter what one may think of unions and their workers: the unavoidable fact is that we will never be able to pay the amount of future benefits the sweetheart contracts commit us to. Those contracts will either be renegotiated or simply abrogated. They will not be fulfilled, because they can't be fulfilled.

Unrealistic labor contracts of this type, where legislators through a financial conflict of interest have not represented the public interest in a negotiation, can only occur where the legislators are both sympathetic to and financially supported by the public-sector unions. Thus the worst excesses of this type have occurred in pro-labor states like New York, Illinois and California. It doesn't work in states where most of the legislators are not fond of unions to begin with.

Unfair pro-corporate contracts – where legislators find themselves in negotiations representing the interests of the corporations who donate to them, rather than the public who elected them – occur in all the states, not least California. Once upon a time it was the Big Five and railroads throwing their weight around in Sacramento. Now it's AT&T and Big Tech.

Why aren't there conflict-of-interest laws enforcing the most basic fiduciary obligations on public officials, especially legislators? Because it is the legislators who would have to pass those laws, thus depriving themselves of the personal benefit they receive by taking money from the parties they're supposed to be negotiating against.

A carefully worded ballot measure might pass, but can you imagine the opposition? It would be one of the few cases in history where unions and corporations would vie to outspend one another on the same side of an issue.

It might be the courts where the public has the best future chance of having fiduciary obligations imposed on our public officials. To understand how, let's return to our example of hiring an agent to sell the family farm. Suppose you followed your agent's advice and sold it cheap, to someone you later found out had paid your agent well to convince you to act against your interests. In court you would have a good chance, not only of having the transaction reversed and getting your farm back, but receiving damages from both your ex-agent and the buyer he colluded with.

Analogously, the public has an arguable case that many of the contracts our legislators have saddled us with – sweetheart on their face, because of their lopsided terms – resulted from the conflicts of interest inherent in receiving money from parties they're supposedly negotiating against. Those sweetheart contracts should be set aside as invalid, and laws should be created that disallow any parties who negotiate with the public to donate money or provide personal benefit to any public official.

May 30, 2012
MONEY IN POLITICS: WHY WE ARE WHERE WE ARE

Money has always played a supporting role in politics, but as anyone following the news during this election cycle can attest, money is now vying for the starring role. The subject of this thread is how we got here – in particular the general principles and judicial reasoning underlying our laws governing money in politics. The legal landscape has shifted over the last decades, and shows every sign of continuing to be a work-in-progress. By identifying the underpinnings that support the laws we now have, we can clarify our own beliefs on the subject, and maybe even predict in what direction future laws might evolve.

The good news is that almost the entire welter of money-in-politics law is supported by a very few core doctrines. Here are the major pillars:

1. In a democracy, quid pro quo arrangements – where a public official does something for someone or some group in return for money or other material benefit – are corrupt. Since such exchanges are often difficult to detect and prove, policies should be in place that actively discourage their occurrence.

2. Groups (corporations and unions) have greater potential to corrupt public officials than do individuals.

3. The First Amendment prohibits government from rationing, balancing, proportioning, metering, or otherwise limiting political speech, or the money spent to disseminate it.

4. Campaign contributions, expenditures, and other monies spent on political speech are private, not public, benefits, in that they benefit the candidates or speakers, not the public at large.

5. Foreign governments, corporations and individuals should be restricted from participating in our political process, by prohibiting them from making campaign contributions or engaging in political advocacy.

Now let's look at how these core values are applied to our money-in-politics laws.

1. The acknowledgment that quid pro quo (aka "pay to play") exchanges are corrupt is why we have campaign contribution limits. Since the dollar threshold where corruption becomes plausible depends on the public office, limits differ for the various federal, state and local offices, and they are adjusted over time. The same reasoning results in limits or bans on lobbying gifts. Unfortunately, the many allowable exceptions for lobbying gifts and favors make those laws as airtight as swiss cheese.

Laws requiring disclosure of the identities of campaign donors and activities of lobbyists are also based on the notion of quid pro quo corruption. We can't very well identify corruption if we don't know who gave or did what when. Some have argued that donors should have a right to anonymity, to protect against retribution. Prevailing Supreme Court majority opinion is that it is more important to know the identity of contributors, than to give them the protection of anonymity.

Not long ago the Supreme Court majority showed in another case how far it would go to prioritize protections against quid pro quo corruption, when it struck down a law that allowed a candidate to enjoy higher campaign contribution limits, when facing a wealthy opponent who self-financed beyond a certain threshold. The controlling factor here was the increased risk of quid pro quo corruption if exceptional limits were permitted in some circumstances.

Since quid pro quo corruption requires an exchange between an individual (or group) and another, a candidate self-financing his or her own campaign cannot commit quid pro quo corruption, and is thus not limited in how much money he or she can self-contribute.

Similarly, quid pro quo corruption is not possible in a ballot measure, because there is not a candidate to be corrupted, but a proposition to be voted up or down. For that reason contributions to organizations advocating for or against the measure are not subject to limits.

2. Some readers may be surprised that corporations and unions are often prohibited from making direct campaign contributions to candidates or public officials, since there is so much talk about their 'buying' and 'owning' politicians. Unfortunately, this is another example of legal swiss cheese. Note that I quietly slipped in the word 'direct' in the sentence above. While a corporation or union can't donate directly, they can form a political action committee or 527 and contribute that way. Why the painfully obvious sleight-of-hand? Why, if we acknowledge that groups shouldn't be allowed to directly contribute to candidates because of the increased risk of corruption,

do we allow them to indirectly contribute the same amounts through PACs and 527s?

3. The third principle is more about political speech than candidate campaigns, and it's what was primarily at issue in the recent Citizens United case. Majorities on the Supreme Court for some time now have evolved toward interpreting the First Amendment such that government has no authority to decide how much political speech any group or individual is entitled to. A series of rulings have shaped this core doctrine.

For example, campaigns, either for public office or a ballot measure, are not restricted in the total amounts of money they may spend. Campaign contribution limits for candidate donors, yes, but a limit on how much any campaign itself can spend, or at what rate? No. Political speech can't be capped or metered.

The Supreme Court in Citizens United struck down a Michigan law they had once upheld, that placed certain restrictions on corporations, but not on unions. The majority now reasoned that government could not play favorites, or adjust the tilt of a playing field, when it came to political speech. Restrictions on speech or the money spent to broadcast it can't be used as a balance or lever to compensate for other perceived inequities.

Citizens United also removed some of the last restrictions on group political speech made independent of a campaign for public office. Congress's latest iteration of campaign finance reform (2002) had a provision that restricted groups from trying to influence who you vote for in the period leading up to an election. A group called Citizens United complained to the FEC after the 2004 election that Michael Moore had violated the provision with his anti-Bush movie "Fahrenheit 9/11." There was some confusion over whether the film or its trailers had been shown in the forbidden pre-election period, but the FEC found in the substantive part of its ruling that Moore's movie was a commercial enterprise anyway, not primarily a screed against Bush.

Citizens United did something interesting after they lost the case. They started making full-length documentary movies. The one that landed them in front of the Supreme Court was an anti-Hillary film. What they were insisting on was their right to show the movie on Directv, for similar reasons Michael Moore enjoyed. They weren't challenging the law's provision per se, just insisting on its uniform application.

When the case was heard, the Solicitor General over-argued that the provision actually gave the government more authority to restrict political speech than it was currently exercising. He gave some scary hypothetical examples, like banning books and e-books, that implied expansive untapped powers of prior restraint. His overstepping opened the door to wider questions from justices who already disliked the provision itself, not just how it was being applied.

A Supreme Court soap opera ensued behind closed doors in the months that followed, resulting finally in a second hearing before the Supreme Court on the same case. This time the provision itself was on the chopping block. One of the arguments the prevailing majority employed was that a whole class of corporation – those owning media outlets like newspapers, magazines, websites, tv and radio stations – were allowed to tell the public how to vote right up to the moment they stepped into the voting booth. In fact it is a time-honored tradition for a newspaper corporation to earnestly advise us how to vote on every item on every ballot, and those recommendations wield vast, often decisive, influence. Why should other corporations and unions be restricted in their political speech, when media corporations get to say whatever they want whenever they want?

That argument won the day, and we're experiencing the full effects now during the first post-Citizens United presidential election cycle. The only real restriction is that the group must be independent of – not coordinated with – any candidate's campaign, again to guard against quid pro quo corruption.

4. When you contribute to a candidate, or political party, or political action committee, your contribution is not tax-deductible. That's because the law considers the money to go to the private benefit of the candidate or party or committee. While the law is extremely generous in what it is willing to allow an organization to believe or allege is in the public interest, candidate and other ballot-related political contributions are toward someone or some group's private interest.

Conversely, a non-profit public interest corporation like a 501, or a church or other religious institution, is not allowed to directly participate in candidate politics. Since non-profits and churches receive their money tax-free (not as income), and donors can deduct their donations from taxable income, they cannot use that money for a private interest like electoral politics.

It is somewhat less legally clear in the wake of Citizens United why non-profits and churches can't express their political opinions, independent of campaigns, as everyone else is now entitled to do, in those instances where the expression of opinion does not require a direct financial expense (like buying an ad). Since the prohibition against politics from the pulpit has been observed in the breach for decades, it may not be too much longer for this world.

5. You will not find any full-page New York Times ads taken out by foreign governments telling you how to vote. Not that they wouldn't like to directly influence the outcome of elections, but our laws consider that all of our elections reflect our national interest. Since foreign corporations and individuals can also be assumed to have their national interest in their home country, and every national interest (even in the case of close allies) is distinct from and potentially opposed to any other national interest, we systematically exclude non-American elements from participation in our political process.

One questionable aspect of this policy: where a corporation happens to be registered, or headquartered, or what stock exchange it is traded on, is not a very reliable indicator of its national makeup or allegiance. It is often simply a business decision. There is an undeniable quaintness to the notion that we feel so protected by the sometimes incidental fact that a multinational corporation is registered and located here, that we grant it broad rights to participate in our political process.

October 19, 2010
CAMPAIGN CONTRIBUTIONS: FOREIGN, ANONYMOUS, NEFARIOUS?

Last week the White House accused the U.S. Chamber of Commerce of using money from foreign sources to finance electoral campaign ads. The White House blamed the fact that contributions can be anonymous for its inability to produce any incriminating evidence. Two underlying public policy questions arise:

1. Why is it illegal to make and receive campaign contributions from foreign sources?

2. Should it be illegal to make and receive anonymous campaign contributions?

The first question can be approached by looking at existing U.S. law governing foreign activity in our electoral campaigns. The purpose of the law, first passed in 1966 and governed by the Federal Elections Commission, is to "minimize foreign intervention in U.S. elections" by "foreign nationals." A foreign national includes foreign governments, political parties, corporations, associations, partnerships, individuals of foreign citizenship, and U.S. immigrants without a green card.

The reason we attempt to restrict foreign nationals from unduly influencing our elections is because their national interests can never be identical to our own. It doesn't matter whether the foreign national is sympathetic to the U.S., or our worst enemy. In every case it is assumed that a foreign national's interests are always necessarily distinguishable from our national interests. For that reason neither the government of

Canada nor North Korea can take out, or subsidize, an ad in the New York Times to tell us how to vote. Unlike North Korea, Canadian interests may be largely aligned with ours, but they can never be identical. Canadian loyalties literally lie elsewhere.

If "money is speech," as Justice Scalia pithily wrote, then in the case of foreign nationals we restrict their free speech vis-à-vis our elections insofar as we restrict foreign nationals' ability to spend or give money to influence our elections. In other words, in this case it is more important to protect our elections from foreign manipulation, than to protect foreign nationals' free speech.

The problem with this line of reasoning is that it applies equally to all corporations, even if they are headquartered in the U.S., or traded on an American stock exchange. Corporations of a certain size today are generally multinational in scope, operating in many countries, owned at least in part by foreign nationals. Whether a multinational corporation designates itself "American" is largely a business decision based on a variety of financial factors. A corporation's self-interests – wherever it is located and doing business – are to survive and maximize profits: it is difficult to imagine a circumstance where a corporation's interests would be identical with any country's national interests. Perhaps if the government wholly owned the corporation.

Otherwise the same rationale that causes us to restrict foreign nationals' participation in our elections applies equally well to all corporations. A corporation – American or foreign – is loyal to itself, to its survival and success; it is not necessarily patriotic or loyal to any particular government or country or national interests.

What about other American organizations, like political parties, or special interest associations, or even individual Americans themselves? Can they be assumed to have enough skin in the American game, such that their organizational and personal interests are necessarily patriotic, aligned and identical with our national interests? We may wish that to be true, while knowing it is not.

Bottom line: the yardstick we use for restricting foreign influence in our elections – that foreigners predictably have loyalties distinct from our national interests – applies equally well to American corporations, organizations, and even individuals. Go figure.

A better reason to restrict foreign influence over our elections might be the corollary to the Golden Rule. As Americans, we never attempt to influence foreign elections (really?). So stay out of ours.

The second question, whether we should permit anonymous political contributions or expenditures, is like the frosting on the first question. It would be bad enough for the Chinese government to tell us how to vote. To do so secretly through a third party, to anonymously puppeteer the players in our elections, would be doubly nefarious. Not only would foreign nationals be exercising undue influence over our elections, they would be doing so without our knowledge.

Of course anonymity can present the same problem, regardless of the puppeteer. In electoral campaigns, we want to hear the message, and to know who financed the message, that is, to identify the messenger. Presumably that will have some impact upon how we perceive the validity of the message.

There's the nub of the argument against anonymity: our perception of the message is impacted by our knowledge of the identity of the messenger. This is a questionable benefit, since the veracity of a message should be determinable independent of knowledge of the messenger's identity. In fact it can be argued that a more objective determination would be arrived at without such knowledge.

While the benefit of prohibiting anonymity is questionable, the political cost is undeniable. Without anonymity, no one can financially support any cause, no matter how unpopular, without the government's and general public's knowledge. As our history has proven too many times, support of politically unpopular causes or organizations can be very dangerous to your health. Chances are that when you know your financial support for an unpopular cause will be known to the government, you'll take a pass. And the worse the government's retribution against those it disfavors, the more likely you'll take that pass. Score one for social conformity, the status quo, and in the worst cases, tyranny.

Use this website as a test case. We all know that allowing anonymity has encouraged all manner of antisocial misbehavior. Some people haven't even felt the need for anonymity to behave antisocially.

That's the downside. On the upside, people can anonymously express ideas that are unpopular, even dangerously unpopular. That may not seem like such an important right in a relatively stable, safe, sane society. The ability to anonymously express ideas would seem like a very big deal in a society staring into the abyss.

October 25, 2011
NEUTRALIZING THE INFLUENCE OF MONEY OVER POLITICS

Efforts to control the influence of money over politics have thus far been a spectacular failure, as the status quo will richly attest. So let's start by looking at what's been tried, and why it's failed.

To make a long sordid story fairly short, the Congress, state legislatures, counties and municipalities passed a series of laws over the last decades that limited the amount of money that individuals or groups could contribute to an electoral campaign. They also placed limits on a campaign's total expenditures, on a candidate's self-spending, and on non-campaign (outside money) spending for or against a candidate or ballot measure.

Most of that legislation has been found unconstitutional by the Supreme Court, in a series of rulings that revolve around the notion that to limit an individual or group's ability to spend on political speech, is tantamount to limiting the act of political speech itself. That position (known colloquially as "money=speech") makes spending limits a First Amendment violation.

One major exception has been allowed. The Supreme Court, recognizing that the government has a compelling interest in discouraging corruption of public officials, has allowed limits on the amount of money that any one individual or group can contribute to a candidate. There are a lot of ways around this restriction, but there it is. Pretty much the sum total of what the Supreme Court finds constitutional in campaign finance reform.

As observers of the electoral landscape have noticed, authorities are always playing a losing game of political whack-a-mole with campaigns and groups over the rules. Nothing stimulates the human mind like the opportunity to bend a rule to the breaking point, making campaign finance law avoidance one of the most creative endeavors ever. You know, soft money, 527s, super-PACs, etc.

Another big problem with enforcement is the absence of meaningful penalties. When is the last time you heard of a successful candidate being withheld or removed from office because his campaign violated a campaign finance statute, or something subject to judicial interpretation, like bashing an opponent with lying ads in the days before the election? Penalties are mostly small pecuniary slaps on the wrist, a mere cost of doing modern-day politics. Bottom line: the laws aren't a deterrent.

The proper way around the Supreme Court is a constitutional amendment. Sounds good, except the devil's in the details. For example, we could mandate that all electoral campaigns are to be entirely public-financed. But a potential candidate has to spend money to do practically everything necessary to begin and develop the campaign process, to get his or her name and platform out there. Public money would only kick in at a certain point. We can't fully finance from Day One the activities of every person who thinks they'd make a good public official.

The greater problem is the prospect of restricting everyone else's ability to spend private money in order to express their political preferences. We can't exercise prior restraint against everyone, both because it violates everything we believe about free speech and it's utterly impractical.

My reworking of the Constitution, called Re-Constitution, takes a different approach to campaign reform. Rather than telling campaigns and the public what they can't do (inevitably restricting speech and forever playing a losing game of whack-a-mole), Re-Con requires candidates to go through a rigorous, mandatory public process that is designed to expose a candidate to full public scrutiny. Think of it as the mother of all job applications, or a reality show structured to tell us everything we could possibly need or want to know about the candidates. If we had that public process, no amount of private spending on attack ads and fluff pieces would appreciably influence our voting.

As an example of the process, can you imagine what it would be like to watch candidates for President take an essay exam on live TV, answering unrehearsed questions from the public audience? The effect of having them reading their verbatim answers, and then answering verbal follow-up questions, with all the results replayed and reprinted for everyone to see and absorb? No amount of money could spin the results (or more likely, erase the damage). Just an example.

September 23, 2011
HOW AMERICA COULD BECOME A DEMOCRACY

First, the good news: we have the right economic system. Call it capitalism, free enterprise, or a market economy, it's the one most people want. We know that, because almost a century of non-market, planned, state-run economies have been tried and failed – people literally voted with their feet. The problem with the soviet-style command economy was that it robbed people of the personal initiative to better themselves financially. There's no market outlet for entrepreneurialism, the great instinctive natural engine of capitalism.

The question that remains unsolved is how best to politically run this ideal economic system. In America, we have democratic and republican forms – primarily because we can vote – but in reality we have the substance of a plutocracy: individuals and organizations with greater wealth can easily exercise greater political influence. Experts from Plato to James Madison found the 'wealth=political influence' equation perfectly acceptable, even desirable. There are some flies in the plutocratic ointment however, which we are experiencing right now, in the still fairly adolescent life of our country.

Think of an economy as a competition between everyone, like the natural competition that occurs between creatures in the sea, or on land, because that's really what it is. Like natural competitions, there is a kind of food chain to our market economy. At the top of the food chain, we have the entities that acquire or aggregate substantial wealth. These are both individuals and groups of individuals, like corporations, trusts, unions, etc. The middle of our economic food chain is occupied by people with decent jobs, comfortable retirees, etc. You know, the proverbial middle class. The lower echelons of our capitalist food chain are occupied by people in dead-end jobs, the unemployed and underemployed, and finally at the bottom, the homeless and the unemployable.

When spelled out like that it's clear enough that where you are in the economic food chain pretty much determines where you are in the political food chain. Different parts of the food chain have different political options. If you're near the bottom of the food chain and oppose a policy, you might write a letter or go to a street demonstration. If you're near the top of the food chain, you or your lobbyist meet the politician at a fundraiser, or over dinner. What's so wrong with that? Isn't that the natural order of things?

To answer the question, it's important to be frank with ourselves about a certain uncomfortable truth: that with precious few exceptions, people and groups of people act politically in their own self-interests. Not the larger interests of their nation, or class, or community, or whatever, but in their necessarily narrow self-interests. What we are experiencing now is a political system where entities with wealth are disproportionately exercising what they perceive to be their own self-interests, in competition with everyone else, including other entities with wealth.

One aspect that distinguishes our human economic competition from a more animal struggle for survival, is that we have rules – called laws – which reflect an understanding of how this grand game of human survival should be played. And like any game with rules, many (most?) participants are perfectly happy to bend or break the rules, if it serves their self-interests and they can get away with it. So we have to police the game: without a government referee capable of enforcing the rules, they will largely be observed in the breach.

And there is the problem: the moneyed entities that are struggling to financially prevail against one another and all comers, are the same entities that are responsible for creating (or dismantling) the rules of the game. It's not always in their interests to have, or especially follow, the rules. Their self-interest is to prevail financially. Because they do not act as a class, with the self-preservation instincts of their entire class at heart, they compete among themselves and against the other conflicting interests in society. Think of our current economic crisis: it was largely created by relaxed/unenforced financial laws that allowed the flourishing of fugazi mortgage instruments. Trillions of dollars of fugazi instruments.

A better alternative is to have a political system of competition that is designed to allow all sectors of society to prosecute their political self-interests, on an even playing field. That is, a scenario where political influence is deliberately decoupled from economic influence. Then all our self-interests are thrown in the political blender, and we end up with a more stable society that reflects a fair competition between differing but reconcilable interests. Under that scenario, it is more likely that we will have effective and enforceable rules governing our economic competition, so that it is a fairer game of life. The confidence engendered by fair, enforceable rules of business tends to ensure continuing demand and investment.

That is exactly the opposite of what we have today. We call it a 'depression' because today (like in the 1920s and '30s) the rules governing our economy are perceived as slipshod and unfair. The game, like a casino with a bad reputation, pushes people away. Discouraged by the lack of a fair-seeming game to play, people become afraid to spend or invest their money. The depression will likely continue until that perception changes.

For those who agree we need a political system that fairly blends the self-interests of all sectors of society, the primary illusion is that either the Democratic or Republican parties can further that goal. The two major parties are both controlled by, and represent the interests of, the entities of wealth described above. The top of the economic food chain. Where they disagree is how tactically to further their often opposing interests. It is interesting to note that the two parties have oscillated back-and-forth over the many decades, sometimes effecting a full role reversal in their relative positions. When I was a kid, it was Democrats who blocked blacks from entering white schools. A half century before that, the Republicans were trust-busting, and before that, fighting a war against slavery. The Democrats were for states' rights, the Republicans for more centralized national power. Things change and rearrange, but the two parties have become increasingly dominated by larger and larger financial players, who necessarily prosecute their self-interests to the exclusion of all else, as frankly we all have an inclination to do.

The second great illusion is that a fair blending of self-interests can occur under our present Constitution, and especially under its interpretation by the Supreme Court. While it is theoretically possible to amend the Constitution to improve its ability to frame a system that is qualitatively more democratic and republican, it would be more efficient to convene a second Constitutional Convention. The principles behind the parchment can be largely carried over to a new document, with all the modernization and specificity we so sorely need to carry us into a successful future.

Advocacy of this goal would be best achieved by creation of a third political party – call it the New America Party – whose central plank would be the call for a second Constitutional Convention, to create a more truly democratic and republican political system.

October 21, 2011
HOW MUCH DEMOCRACY DO WE HAVE? HOW MUCH DO WE WANT?

This writer and most readers are of course in favor of democracy, in general, and believe we need more of it. The question for this essay: when might we have too much democracy? Is it possible to have too much of such a good thing?

First, we need to define our terms. Democracy ('rule of the people') is a surprisingly difficult concept to nail down in the abstract, so let's look at a practical situation, and find the essentially democratic characteristics within it.

Imagine a group of people, who want to manage themselves as democratically as possible. That would mean – I think we can all agree – that the group would be able to vote on all issues that affect the group, that each member of the group would have one vote, that the votes would be weighted equally, that a simple majority of votes would decide the issue, and the will of the majority would be imposed. Let's call that pure democracy.

You immediately start to see the problems with that scenario. What if a majority of the group decided to condemn you to death, simply because (like Socrates) you were a pain in the neck? That's what John Stuart Mill coined the "tyranny of the majority." There are all sorts of things we don't want the group to decide about individuals or subgroups (minorities), and that's where our concept of rights comes from. A right is something you're entitled to, whether the group wants you to have it or not. The complicating factor is that at some point in a group's history, they had to get together and decide that a 'right' should exist, often for the duration of the group's existence.

Our political system has quite a few situations where 1) some people's votes count more than others, and/or 2) a simple majority cannot impose its will. Then there are the situations where the people don't get to vote at all. Here's a partial list of situations where pure democracy is conspicuously avoided:

• The Senate. As a Californian, because of the size of the state, your personal representation in the Senate is far weaker than someone's from a smaller state. As states, the votes are equal. As persons, the votes are incredibly unequal. This means you have unequal representation on all Senate business, including bills, impeachments, expulsions, vetoes, confirmations of federal nominees (judges, justices, officers, cabinet members, ambassadors, etc.), proposal of constitutional amendments, and treaties. The House of Representatives is specifically excluded from voting on treaty ratifications, nominee confirmations, and impeachment trials.

The Senate also has many examples where a simple majority does not prevail. These include cloture (60/100), vetoes (2/3), impeachments (2/3), expulsions (2/3), treaties (2/3), presidential inability to discharge duties (2/3), and proposed constitutional amendments (2/3 for both houses).

• The Electoral College. As Californians, it's a sorry truth that a lot of us could skip the next presidential election and not affect the outcome. Neither party will spend much money in the state, because the outcome is a foregone conclusion. In fact, only a handful of states are competitive each election cycle. Also, Electoral College votes are weighted unequally toward the smaller states, since their number is arrived at by combining the number of a state's Senators and Representatives. If no candidate receives a majority of Elector votes, the president is chosen in the House, where each state gets one vote (again advantaging the smaller states). Not much democracy, pure or otherwise, in the Electoral College.

• The judicial system. Would we want pure democracy, simple majority rules, on juries? Right now, one person can confound the will of eleven others in criminal trials. Would we want a jury system where a simple majority (determined maybe by one or two swing votes) decides our fate in criminal court?

Another judicial example where a majority's will can be thwarted by a minority is in the granting of judicial review on appeal (certiorari, or 'cert'). For the Supreme Court, it only takes four Justices to grant cert. The other five might not want to hear the appeal, but they have to. Similar provisions exist for the lower federal courts.

• The District of Columbia. DC residents get pretty well aced out of any federal democracy. They have no voting representation in either the Senate or House. They do get Electoral College votes, the minimum allowed, regardless of DC population.

• Ratification of the Constitution. The Framers decided that two-thirds of the states (9/13), not a simple majority, would be required to enact the Constitution.

There are lots of other examples in our political system where pure democracy is clearly avoided. People will disagree about which ones have turned out to be good ideas, but there should be no disagreement that a chemically pure democracy is not something to be desired.

May 23, 2012
WHAT REAL HEALTH CARE REFORM MIGHT LOOK LIKE

Next week the Supreme Court will either uphold, jigger, strike down, or simply carve the beating heart out of Obamacare. After that a mass political psychosis will shortly commence, affecting almost everyone, cresting in November and then settling in for the long haul. The condition will undoubtedly fester because none of the 'solutions' to our health care crisis offered by any of the usual suspects is worthy of the name. They all think a fancy new kind of bandaid will cure a broken leg.

So this might be a good opportunity, before the media madness pollutes us, to try to sort through what reasonable people might do to clean up our health care mess. There are many, many problems, large and small. Let's stick to the herd of elephants in the living room.

A REIMBURSEMENT (CLAIMS-BASED) BUSINESS MODEL FOR MEDICINE IS LITERALLY UNHEALTHY

Insured medical care is like a three-ring circus. First, you have us, the patients. We might have an individual insurance policy for ourselves or our family, or we might have insurance through a group, like an employer or association plan. That's the first circus ring. Then there are the medical care providers: everyone working in the hospitals, clinics and offices, the people who actually take care of us. That's the second ring. The third ring is the insurance company who holds our policy, and reimburses the providers for medical services performed.

Patients, providers, insurers. Typically three separate entities. When we need medical care, we go to the hospital or doctor, who performs medicine on us, then sends a form to our insurance company to be reimbursed. The form the medical provider fills out has hundreds of different codes for the hundreds of different kinds of procedure that might be performed. In other words, the medical provider is being reimbursed almost without exception for procedures performed on us, because those procedures can be defined and described in a uniform way that standardizes reimbursement. While we call what we have "health care insurance," in most cases it would more accurately be termed "medical procedure insurance."

Under this scenario, other than the office visit, the only billable events for a provider are procedures, and of course the more procedures, the more billable events. Preventative medicine under the reimbursement model is not a billable event: there is no procedure code for prevention. On the contrary, the sicker we are, or the more procedures the provider can think of, the greater the revenue stream. Many of us have experienced the insured office visit where the doctor seemed positively eager to recommend procedures that weren't clearly necessary: it's the only way he or she gets paid by the insurance company.

The reimbursement model is deeply entrenched in our medical 'system,' and responsible for many of its deformities. For example, because the model rewards procedures over prevention, most medical students point themselves away from lower-paid career paths like primary or family medicine, and toward higher-paid specialties. So we have a nationwide shortage of primary-care generalists – the early-detection and prevention experts – and plenty of secondary and tertiary acute-care specialists.

A claims-based model is also widely used in Medicare and Medicaid, so that care for the elderly or the poor focuses on procedures, rather than preventive and quality-of-life techniques, like supervision, education, and behavior modification.

To fathom how the reimbursement model dominates our thinking, consider the expression "single payer," which has been popularized by advocates of a particular type of government-run health care system. Now, there are lots of different types of government-run health care systems across the planet. Some governments own all of the hospitals and facilities, and all of the medical personnel are government employees. Most systems are hybrids, involving melds of government, employers, private enterprise, etc. What government-run systems tend to have in common is that they are financed in whole or the greater part by government revenue, primarily taxes, and that there is some level of universally guaranteed care.

"Single payer" means that the government would be the sole ('single') reimburser ('payer') of medical providers. Meaning that the entire system would run on the same reimbursement model we now have. The big difference would be that rather than us buying insurance from companies, the government would pay our medical expenses through taxes and other revenue.

The defects of the reimbursement model would remain.

FOR-PROFIT INSURERS AND NON-PROFIT PROVIDERS: SQUARE PEG, ROUND HOLE

Before describing an alternative to the reimbursement model, we should pause to consider the culture chasm that typically divides our health care providers from our health care insurers, and the problems that chasm creates.

Most of our hospitals and community clinics are non-profit. Built variously by government, churches, universities, physician and benevolent groups, wealthy benefactors etc., or a combination thereof, they exist to provide medical care, pure and simple. To use the IRS's terminology, they're charitable institutions. Sometimes the hospitals and clinics are a part of a larger network, but more often they stand alone. The smallest providers are office doctors who hang out their business shingle and work alone or in group practice.

Most medical insurers, on the other hand, are usually large for-profit insurance companies, like the kind (and often the same as) the companies that might sell us other forms of insurance (auto, life, property, accident, etc.). They tend to become necessarily large because they are more secure and profitable as they grow their customer base and enjoy economies of scale. In many cases the insurance companies are publicly traded; we can own their stock and be a shareholder.

That brief description underlines the structural disparity between typical providers and insurers.

Smaller vs. larger, non-profit vs. for-profit. Their interests are not aligned, and those tensions create very serious problems for us, the patients.

First, there is the overhead. Many of the people who work in a hospital, clinic, or health insurance company are involved in one aspect or another of the provider/insurer administration interface, either filling out, filing, examining, denying, approving, reviewing, billing and (bring on the lawyers) adjudicating claims. Many of those employees spend their lives on telephone hold, just like we do. The bureaucracy is such an octopus that it often strangles the stand-alone storefront doctor right out of business. While the paperwork involved in the provider/Medicare/Medicaid interface is not quite as bad, it still drives up costs across the board.

Second, there is the uncertainty. When a hospital or other provider performs a procedure on us, even if they have received pre-approval, there is always the possibility that – for whatever reason – the claim will ultimately be denied. There is an ever-present built-in financial incentive to deny a claim. The uncertainty of reimbursement becomes especially serious when a patient needs an expensive procedure done. Providers always want to get pre-approval, but what if the expensive procedure needs to happen sooner than later? Doctors and administrators are torn: perform the procedure without insurance authorization, or risk harming or even losing the patient? This is unfortunately how many people have died, waiting on gurneys in hospital hallways. Cause of death: bureaucracy.

THE INSURER/PROVIDER (A VERTICALLY INTEGRATED PROVIDER, OR 'VIP'): A TWO-RING CIRCUS

Why can't health care providers sell insurance directly to the public, so that there are only two rings to the circus: the patients and a vertically-integrated health care insurer/provider? That's the question Henry J. Kaiser asked himself, and Kaiser Permanente became the answer. Some of the more forward-thinking hospital groups around the country (like Cleveland, HealthPartners, Mayo) are experimenting with one VIP form or another, essentially cutting out the middle man between the provider and patient, by directly providing comprehensive insurance. The different business model causes remarkably different results.

With a VIP, which both sells the insurance and practices the medicine, premiums for service are arrived at by calculating the total estimated costs of serving a population, divided by the size of the population. Patient costs are necessarily lower for a number of reasons. The operation is non-profit, so there are no shareholders to satisfy. All revenues go to operating expenses. And because there is no longer the insurer/provider interface, layers of bureaucracy are eliminated.

The biggest reason a VIP drives down patient costs is because the business model encourages preventive medicine. With a VIP, the patient pays a premium in return for the VIP providing comprehensive medical care. It is in the VIP's interest to prevent disease in their patients, through early detection and intervention, education, etc., rather than try to cure disease later on, a much more expensive and doubtful prospect. The deal is simple: the healthier the VIP keeps the patient, through regular checkups, prevention and early detection/intervention, the lower the cost. The healthy patient lives better and longer, happy to pay his or her premium all the while. Win-win. That's why Kaiser's catchphrase is "Thrive." It fits their business model.

VIPs, like anyone providing insurance, benefit from economies of scale, so the model works better for larger hospital and medical groups. Stand-alone hospitals, clinics and offices would need to participate in umbrella insurance groups, with government kickstarts and backing.

WHY VIPs AND THEIR SUBSCRIBERS SHOULDER THE COSTS OF SERVING THE UNINSURED

A legitimate question to ask is why VIPs haven't flourished thus far, if they're such a great idea. One reason is that the playing field is tilted against them politically, often at the urging of the traditional for-profit insurance industry, which rightly sees VIPs as endangering some very profitable turf.

The disadvantages a VIP faces are not always obvious. For example, one of the chief reasons given for the individual purchase mandate in Obamacare is that the costs of caring for the uninsured are currently shifted back onto the insured. That's not exactly true. They're largely shifted back onto the people who insure directly through their medical provider, like a VIP. Here's how it works.

All medical providers are required to assist anyone needing emergency or urgent care, regardless of their ability to pay. This responsibility normally devolves on hospital emergency rooms. If the hospital is owned by the government, say by a city, or county, or state, or federal government, its public funding will typically build in the costs of treating the uninsured. But what if the hospital is not publicly owned? Who reimburses them?

Often, no one. The only way the hospital can recoup the cost is to raise the premiums on individuals and groups who directly insure through the hospital. It cannot simply raise its reimbursement rates to insurance companies, since those rates are negotiable, and the insurance company does not need to agree to share the costs of caring for the uninsured. That would kill their profits.

To repeat: currently, the only way a hospital can typically recoup uninsured costs is by raising premiums on anyone who directly insures with them. Since Kaiser's business model is based on direct insurance, about 10-20% of a Kaiser premium is calculated to cover uninsured costs. Hospitals who do little or no direct insurance business have limited ability to recoup uninsured costs, and therefore are often reluctant to serve the uninsured. Ambulance drivers learn quickly to avoid the run-around and take their uninsured emergency cases to public hospitals or VIPs like Kaiser, where timely service is more likely than at more elite (and less busy) private hospitals who depend on claims-based reimbursements.

The simple, fair way for all of us to share the costs of serving the uninsured is for providers to be reimbursed by the government for this essential social service. Now that's an example of the reimbursement model that would work just fine. And oddly enough, the first baby step toward a minimum standard of guaranteed universal medical maintenance. Let's take a couple more steps in that direction.

UNIVERSAL BASIC HEALTH CARE, AMERICAN STYLE

None of us wants a society where people are denied basic health care. Yet, that's exactly what we have. Other advanced countries seem to be able to provide a basic level of universal care, but it would be difficult to graft those systems and cultures onto ours. Instead, let's look at one of our states, Hawaii, that does things imperfectly but gets the job done. They use a scattershot technique, which is what we'll need across the country. There is no one silver bullet in a national culture that thrives on market competition, personal choice, and mobility.

Hawaii's central lever to bring almost everyone into the health care tent is an employer mandate to purchase employee medical insurance. There are strong reasons to make this the centerpiece. It's where medical insurance began in our society, because it was the physical work people did that cost them their health and longevity. It made perfect sense that the employer should pay for medical attention they largely created the need for. That's why Kaiser started out serving its shipyard and other industrial workers.

The employer obligation still makes sense, but for slightly different reasons. Employers are the ideal buyers of group health insurance from traditional insurers, and especially VIPs. They aggregate populations that negotiate as a group, and they are extremely cost-conscious. They are also often quality control freaks. They closely compete among themselves, and with the health insurers. They demand and discover the most information about the health care providers and insurers. And the more universal the employer mandate is, the greater and more generalized that competition becomes.

Hawaii has a state-run hospital and insurance program with a wide – but minimal – safety net for the poor. That system is competed with very effectively by Kaiser, despite the state's history of tilting the playing field toward its state system. There are also traditional insurers, who have a much smaller market share in Hawaii than in other states, due to competition from the state and Kaiser systems. Each system has its own social niche, like any market for products. When states have a menu of options – VIPs, state programs, traditional insurers – costs go down and quality goes up. Hawaii, warts (and Spam and melanomas) and all, has one of the highest life expectancies in the world.

State and federal government can get almost everyone inside the tent by doing the following:

• mandate employer health insurance obligations, and watch for loopholes

• encourage non-profit VIPs as needed through tax breaks, subsidies, and insurance umbrella groups for smaller providers

• directly reimburse all providers for basic on-demand services to the indigent and uninsured

- take bids from VIPs and traditional insurers wherever possible for Medicare and Medicaid coverage that is paid for by a per capita insurance premium, not reimbursement; more people will be coverable with better results for the same cost

- allow health insurance to cross state lines, so people can migrate with their policies, premiums adjusted where necessary; a lack of portability discourages economic activity

- government should gather and disseminate copious performance and price data and recordkeeping on all providers and insurers, to increase competition, quality and consumer choice

HEALTH CARE COSTS MORE PRIMARILY BECAUSE WE NEED MORE HEALTH CARE

There, I said it. As a people, we are taking rotten care of ourselves. Unless that changes – unless we stop inflicting chronic diseases on ourselves through smoking, alcohol, drugs, obesity, junk food, lack of exercise, depression, stress, etc. – we will experience spiraling cost inflation if for no other reason than we are creating spiraling demand for chronic, acute and terminal medical care. It is an economic verity that an increase in demand triggers an increase in price.

None of the other changes to our health care system will make much of a difference if we continue to commit a painfully slow and expensive form of collective suicide in the form of the typically indulgent American lifestyle. That is the biggest elephant in the health care living room.

Some of us are taking much worse care of ourselves than the rest, and that's where the lion's share of our health care dollars are going. About 1% of the population burns through about 35% of our medical costs. About 10% of the population accounts for 70% of total costs. That means that the remaining 90% of the population makes do with 30% of the medical money pie.

Many of the people in that 1%, or 10%, are there through no fault of their own. They have contracted a horrible disease for which they bear no responsibility. Unfortunately, many more have had an unmistakable hand in the fate they suffer. That is the sad, avoidable story line of today's American health care mess.

BASIC MEDICAL CARE, NOT HEALTH INSURANCE, SHOULD BE RECOGNIZED AS A CIVIL RIGHT

One of the more interesting aspects of the debate over the universal purchase mandate is the accompanying converse assumption that insurers should be required to insure all comers. We can't very well insist that everyone buy insurance if we don't require insurers to sell it to them, without exception. Yet in all our other forms of insurance, insurers quite understandably have the right to choose whom they insure. Auto insurers might pass over the DUI driver with plenty of tickets and accidents. Life insurers might take a pass on gangbangers and mafiosi. Home insurers will inspect your domicile before they consent. Not all accident and casualty insurers will beat a path to the X-Games, looking for customers.

We arrive therefore at the uncomfortable question of why an insurance company should be required to offer a policy to someone who is clearly ignoring their health, or even acting self-destructively. For example, someone who smokes. We know that there is a greater than average chance that a smoker will acquire chronic comorbidities, leading soon enough to expensive acute care. Under the assumptions that have been made about the universal purchase mandate, every insurer in a certain market would be required to offer a policy to every applicant, regardless of their behavior. Yet no size of payable premium could possibly insulate an insurance company from the predictable costs of certain behaviors, such as smoking.

The other problem with a 'universal sales mandate' is that it doesn't discourage bad behavior. In fact, it reinforces it. If I know that I can behave however I like, and still have health insurance, I am in large part relieved of responsibility for the consequences of my actions. I have been allowed to saddle an insurance company with much of the financial risk for my decisions. A good example of moral hazard, and why insurance companies should not be required to insure absolutely all comers. The last thing the American public needs is another excuse to take poor care of ourselves.

This is a fine line, because people should not be shut out of health insurance because of pre-existing conditions, but that is distinguishable from demonstrable present-tense self-destructive behavior. One thing insurers of all types should not be allowed to do is deny or terminate coverage without demonstrating cause before a neutral, third-party public body, like an insurance adjustment board. The way they effect terminations now is by having annual term contracts, that they may quietly decline to renew without cause. Health insurance contracts should be like an old-fashioned marriage, until death do us part, unless the insurer demonstrates we have created clear cause for health insurance divorce.

March 31, 2012
OBAMACARE: PRAGMATISM VS. PRINCIPLE

This week the arguments defending the individual mandate – whether delivered by government attorneys or Supreme Court justices – repeatedly emphasized one very pragmatic concern: that without a purchase requirement, the uninsured's use of the health care system will continue to unfairly place a cost-shifting burden on those who do pay for medical insurance. According to the argument, the premiums that the insured (or their employers) pay necessarily include the costs of serving the uninsured. Often the costs are very wasteful, as in the unnecessary use of emergency rooms for otherwise routine care. A two-fold problem results: the costs of treating the uninsured are inflated, and the insured then foot the bloated bill. The only practical way to shrink the ranks of the uninsured is to make the purchase of medical insurance a universal legal requirement. So the reasoning goes.

The most noteworthy aspect of this argument is its pragmatism – its focus on solving a very practical cost-containment problem. The problem itself, its causes and scale and trajectory, as well as the proposed solution: all of this is eminently examinable. But before we do a bit of that, let's look at the history of what has happened when a pressing pragmatic argument is urged in the face of traditional constitutional objections.

Normally constitutional disagreements involve varying interpretations of text or precedent, that ultimately represent clashes of constitutional principle. From time to time, some of the most momentous turns in constitutional history have occurred when advocates for one side of the argument presented a pragmatic emergency that only an extraordinary legal innovation would solve. These cases have ushered in some of the more dangerous and damaging developments in our judicial history.

To take an infamous example, when the internment of Japanese-Americans came before the Supreme Court in WWII, the very pragmatic problem that the government presented was that a fifth column would otherwise likely develop among stateside Japanese. The only way to head off a fifth column development was to sequester the entire Japanese-American population. A pragmatic abundance of racist caution won the day, to the Constitution's detriment.

Other solutions that conformed to the Constitution were of course available. We know that, because the presence of a fifth column was much more evident among German-Americans, but no similar effort was made to herd them into camps. We simply monitored the community, and sometimes infiltrated suspected fifth column groups.

More recently, since 9-11 our government attorneys have made a number of pragmatic arguments before the Supreme Court defending indefinite detention, 'enhanced interrogation,' warrantless surveillance, rendition, etc. While the constitutional objections to these varied practices have run the gamut, the government response has always been very pragmatic: we are facing exceptional problems that can only be solved or managed by the unprecedented means under question. In some of these cases, to their credit, the Justices have stood their constitutional ground. This post-9-11 series of pragmatic government arguments before the Supreme Court, where extraordinary circumstances always seem to require Constitution-bending responses, is the historical context in which Obamacare is being considered.

Government attorneys struggled to answer a straightforward question about Obamacare: if persons can be legally required to enter into and make ongoing payments to fulfill a complicated service contract with a necessarily large and powerful medical insurance company, for their entire lives, at current prices that are unregulated, and future prices that are uncertain, what can't people be required by the government to do or purchase, in the purported public interest?

The answer: the purchase mandate is the only way to avoid an unfair $40 billion cost-shift per year. The problem, and the nature of health care, are unique.

Let's take a closer look at that assertion. First, there could be a government-run universal health care system, the one Obama supported throughout his campaign, when he opposed the purchase mandate. No cost-shifting there. Next, the $40B/year figure is questioned far and wide. Even if it were accurate, $40B is a relatively small figure, by government or corporate standards. Congress could require insurance companies and hospitals to absorb the cost of treating the uninsured, and regulate insurance premiums and medical costs like we do public utility rates. It could expand Medicaid, fiscally favor non-profit HMOs, and/or mandate or subsidize low-cost policies for the previously uninsured. It could make it easier for hospitals to collect on the uninsured who could afford to pay for services they've received. It could increase employer insurance requirements. There are lots of things Congress could do – constitutionally – to eliminate the cost-shifting, and minimize the numbers of uninsured.

Since the government's pragmatic argument is based on the unproven premise that if everyone is required to have medical insurance, it will "bend the cost curve down," we should take a closer look at that idea as well. The assertion is that if these necessarily few large for-profit medical insurance corporations have a greatly expanded and guaranteed market of customers, they will enjoy greater economies-of-scale and ... pass the savings on to us, the consumers. Think about it: large corporations, guaranteed a customer base who cannot legally do without medical insurance, will pass any savings along to us, not themselves and their shareholders. Is that what is happening at the gasoline pump, where a handful of enormous corporations have a locked-in customer base? Do you think, as you stand at the pump, that they're passing along their economies-of-scale to us? Why would a medical insurance corporation behave any differently?

Bottom line: there are a lot of creative ways to bring down the cost of health care, and make sure everyone has a medical safety net. Because the system is hemorrhaging, no solution will be painless. But it must be constitutional, regardless of the perceived severity of the problem. Instead, Obamacare has chosen a path that would be a gateway drug for an increasingly oppressive and invasive government.

p.s. Should the Supreme Court strike down only the purchase mandate, or the entire law?

Only the mandate. Why? Even though the mandate has been politically positioned as the bill's linchpin, the keystone without which the law falls apart, that is Congress's problem to sort out. The law is not made unconstitutional in its entirety because a central element is unconstitutional. Its authors purposely left out a severability clause, to raise the political stakes on the Justices. But a body of law is not necessarily unseverable simply because it lacks a severability clause. It is the task of the lawmakers – not the Supreme Court – to sort through what remains.

July 8, 2012

THE FEDERAL GOVERNMENT LACKS CONSTITUTIONAL AUTHORITY TO USE TAXATION TO REGULATE BEHAVIOR

Sounds wrong, doesn't it? Counterexamples would seem to abound. This essay will not however delve deeply into examples of regulatory taxation that Congress or the federal executive has imposed, or how the Supreme Court has interpreted their constitutionality, but rather what the Constitution itself says on the federal taxing power as a regulatory tool. First we'll look at how the issue arrived on today's front burner. Then we'll get into the constitutional weeds, to understand on textual, historical and logical grounds that the title of this essay is true.

CONTEXT: AN ASSERTED POWER TO TAX BEHAVIOR WE CAN'T OTHERWISE REGULATE

Last month Chief Justice Roberts punted the political football/hot potato known as Obamacare back to the other two branches of government. Having agreed that the Commerce Clause does not allow Congress to regulate inactivity, he turned to the Taxing and Spending Clause to give the individual mandate his constitutional blessing. Confronted with the outer limits of a Commerce Clause that steadily expanded through the 20th century, the Chief Justice shifted his rationale to what is alleged to be an even more expansive taxing power.

Dissenting opinion pointed out the obvious: that the law consistently, unambiguously and accurately frames the mandate as a requirement subject to penalty; that its authors understood then and its signer and supporters insist now that the mandate is a penalty; that if it were a tax, it wouldn't be ripe for adjudication until 2014 and later because of the Taxation Anti-Injunction Act; and that the Chief Justice, for political reasons unknown, basically endorsed – not the law itself – but what he imagined to be a functionally equivalent rewrite of Obamacare he made up in his head.

Lost in both the dissent and ensuing media din is an examination of the underlying unproven premise, the assertion that if the mandate is considered a tax subject to exemption – not a requirement subject to penalty – the law is constitutional, even though Congress has no other enumerated power with which to require individuals to purchase medical insurance. As we will see, simply put, Congress has no constitutional authority to use taxation to regulate behavior. Its constitutional authority allows Congress to use taxation to raise revenue, not regulate behavior: specifically, to pay government debt, to spend to protect the country ("common defense"), and to spend to improve the country ("general welfare"). The Constitution says nothing about Congress having a power to coerce (or even discourage) behavior through the threat of increased taxation.

Before we look at the Constitution's tax language, there are some preliminary points to nail down. First, it's important to recognize that a requirement subject to penalty, and a tax subject to exemption, are two different and mutually exclusive categories. The penalty/tax distinction is not like the wave/particle distinction in physics (two aspects of the same thing, considered either as energy or matter). A penalty is a punishment for an unlawful act; a tax is any government charge upon the public.

WHICH IS IT, A TAX OR A PENALTY?

This is the second preliminary point to go over, because there is a great deal of confusion on the question. The most important distinction to observe is that the Supreme Court is the final arbiter in deciding cases; it is not the final arbiter in determining what things are. The best demonstration that the mandate is not a tax is to construct a counterfactual, by designing a law (the one Chief Justice Roberts imagines) where the mandate would actually be implemented as a tax. In that case, beginning in 2014, each tax bracket would go up by 1% for everyone. By 2016, each tax bracket would go up 2.5% for everyone. In order to be exempted from the newly elevated rates, we would present evidence on our tax return that we had purchased medical insurance in that year. You want to pay less tax? Buy medical insurance. Or take out a home mortgage. Or make charitable contributions.

The only difference – and it is crucial – is that in this counterfactual we are imagining a law where the tax rates are raised for everyone, specifically as a surcharge in case one does not have medical insurance. In the real-life examples of mortgage and charitable deductions, we have not passed laws bumping up tax rates as a surcharge for not having a home mortgage or making charitable contributions. We want to encourage home ownership and philanthropy by offering those as possible deductions; in the counterfactual law I have created where the mandate is treated as a tax, we all would automatically owe the surcharge, unless we demonstrate that we have medical insurance.

It is clear why the actual law crafted the mandate as a penalty, not a tax, as in my counterfactual. In that imaginary event, a common middle-class tax rate, such as 15%, would quickly climb to 17.5% in 2016, a politically unpalatable scenario, even if only a small percentage of people (4 million in the first year, by CBO estimates) are not eventually exempted from the surcharge. Nominally higher rates (with exemptions available to medical insurance holders) would show up on everyone's tax form beginning in 2014, and beyond. That would make it a tax, and that won't happen. It just wouldn't look good. So it's a penalty, collected by the IRS. The IRS collects many penalties unrelated to taxation, because it's already set up as the de facto multi-purpose collection agency for the government.

TAXATION TO RAISE REVENUE, AND TAXATION TO REGULATE BEHAVIOR

As a third preliminary point, let's distinguish between two basic types of taxes: those that are designed to raise revenue for the government, so it can pay debt and finance its work, and those that are designed to regulate our behavior, either by encouraging or discouraging (or perhaps coercing) us to do or not do certain actions. Sometimes the same tax primarily raises revenue, and secondarily regulates behavior, or vice versa. A two-fer. A regulatory tax might be disguised as a revenue tax, to avoid the constitutional problems we will uncover.

The government's power to use taxation to raise revenue is formidable. In fact, our national government doesn't use a lot of the power the Constitution gives it. For example, it could use a head tax, or capitation, to (as Chief Justice Roberts puts it) charge people just for being alive. The head tax would need to be uniform (like one price for adults, a discount for kids or elderly, etc.), and it would need to be apportioned among the states (a state with X% of the national population yielding X% of the head tax). We don't have head taxes not because they're not constitutionally permissible, but because they're primitive (one price fits all, rich or poor) and politically unpopular.

The federal government could also collect property tax for revenue purposes, another type of 'direct' tax (like a head tax) that only needs to be uniform and apportioned among the states. The problem with a federal apportioned land tax quickly became apparent: that state and local assessors would undervalue properties to minimize their jurisdiction's resented federal tax burden, and that the federal government would need to send its own army of assessors to all locales to attempt to standardize valuations. So from necessity and by custom, our society has confined property or land taxes to the states, normally to supply locales their principal revenue source. There is also no constitutional prohibition against the federal government collecting a national sales tax, which again by political custom our society leaves to the states and locales.

The point here is that when it comes to levying and collecting taxes to raise revenue, the federal government has virtually unrestricted power to tax just about everything that moves, and everything that doesn't. While most people only experience federal taxation through income tax, there is an almost endless list of ways the federal government uses taxation to generate revenue. All it basically needs to do is make sure that the tax is uniform, and apportioned among the states where required.

On the other hand, a good example of a regulatory tax is the large excise we place on cigarettes and alcohol. While we may pretend that the taxes are primarily there to pay society's smoking- and drinking-related expenses, the primary reason we heavily tax cigarettes and alcohol is to discourage people from smoking and drinking. A good example of a revenue tax that could have a regulatory component is a gasoline tax. Gas taxes primarily provide government revenue to pay society's driving-related expenses, like building and maintaining roads. A policy that also wished to discourage driving would simply raise the gas tax to a level designed to depress demand.

For some tax laws, judicial interpretation would be required to determine whether revenue or regulation is the primary purpose. That problem of interpretation does not exist for Obamacare, as the penalties for individuals who don't carry medical insurance (referred to now by the White House as "freeloaders"), and for employers with more than 50 employees who do not offer medical insurance, are so small that they cannot be considered to be designed to generate revenue sufficient to cover the costs to government of "freeloader" behavior.

REFERENCES TO TAXATION IN THE CONSTITUTION, ARTICLES OF CONFEDERATION, AND DECLARATION OF RIGHTS

The Constitution is a document of few words when it comes to taxation. It mentions in Article I, Section 9 that capitation and other direct taxes need to be apportioned among the states, as discussed above. We have the 16th amendment from 1913 that allows taxation of all incomes. And then we have the Taxing and Spending Clause (Article I, Section 8), the all-important first item from the list of enumerated congressional powers:

"The Congress shall have power to lay and collect taxes, duties, imposts and excises, to pay the debts and provide for the common defense and general welfare of the United States...."

The taxing power was probably listed first among Congress's powers, because it was precisely the crucial power that Congress lacked under the Articles of Confederation, which treated the subject in its Article VIII:

"All charges of war, and all other expenses that shall be incurred for the common defense or general welfare, and allowed by the United States in Congress assembled, shall be defrayed out of a common treasury, which shall be supplied by the several states...."

The reader will notice that the "common defense" and "general welfare" language of our Constitution is lifted verbatim from the Articles of Confederation, where the phrases are linked directly and solely to the defraying of government expenses.

Further textual evidence that the Founders and Framers considered the sole purpose of taxation to be the generation of government revenue, can be found in the 1774 Declaration of Rights, the famously unsuccessful letter that the Continental Congress addressed to king and Parliament. In the Declaration, each reference to taxation weds it to revenue:

- The first sentence of the document refers to "expressly imposed taxes...for the purpose of raising a revenue...."

- The fourth Resolve complains of "taxation, internal or external, for raising a revenue on the subjects in America, without their consent."

- The eleventh Resolve refers to the imposition of "duties for the purpose of raising a revenue...."

The Founders and Framers simply did not articulate a lawful purpose for taxation, other than the generation of revenue, in the key documents establishing our nation.

JEFFERSON/MADISON VS. HAMILTON ON THE TAXING AND SPENDING CLAUSE

The first big fight over interpretation of the newly ratified Constitution centered on the Taxing and Spending Clause. Secretary of the Treasury Alexander Hamilton proposed a number of fiscal measures – assumption of state debt, redemption of that and other debt at full face value (par), creation of a national bank, and taxes to finance such policies – citing the Taxing and Spending Clause (as well as its Section 8 bookend, the Necessary and Proper Clause) as an enumerated power authorizing the measures.

Secretary of State Thomas Jefferson and Virginia Representative James Madison saw the Taxing and Spending Clause differently. For them, it was a preamble to the listed powers, not a power in itself, so that Congress could tax and spend based only on the specific enumerated powers that followed. Their concern was that otherwise the Taxing and Spending Clause would be too open-ended, allowing Congress to tax and spend for just about any purpose, as long as it paid debt, or plausibly provided for the common defense or general welfare. They thought, for example, that a constitutional amendment would be needed to enumerate the power to create a national bank. This battle raged down the decades, as factions debated the constitutionality of "internal improvements" bills for "general welfare" items like roads, canals, harbors, etc.

Hamilton's understanding prevailed over time, chiefly because our specific future needs can never be fully foreseen and exhaustively enumerated. If Congress lacked the power to tax and spend on the general welfare as it reasonably sees fit, it couldn't spend to finance things like the Smithsonian, or a national zoo, or non-military space travel, and on and on, without going through the unwieldy process of constitutional amendment. One line-in-the-sand we've paid lip service to is that states retain so-called police powers – over the health, safety, welfare and morals of its inhabitants – confining congressional activity to spending on the general, that is national, welfare. To give them their due, Madison and Jefferson were correct to warn that this "loose construction" of the Taxing and Spending Clause would create a federal behemoth.

The purpose of revisiting this history is to underscore the fact that at no time in the famous debate over the Taxing and Spending Clause did either faction advocate a constitutional power to use taxation for purposes other than raising and spending revenue. Their concern was simply how broadly taxing and spending that revenue on "general welfare" could be construed.

Our concern today is light years beyond, and entirely different: we have now to ask ourselves how far the government is willing to go to use taxation to make us behave as it wishes. We have seen that there is no textual authority in our founding documents for regulatory taxation. We have also seen that the historical characters (even the redoubtable Hamilton), who fought over taxing and spending powers as the constitutional ink dried, didn't recognize taxation as a tool to regulate behavior. Now let's look at the logic of the situation: whether any meaningful limitations would remain on a federal government that the Constitution expressly designed to be limited in its powers, if taxation can indeed be used to regulate our actions.

IF TAXATION CAN BE USED TO MANDATE THE PURCHASE OF MEDICAL INSURANCE, WHAT ELSE BY INFERENCE COULD BE MANDATED?

The 'doomsday' scenario that the government could make us buy broccoli (which even gets a few mentions in the Supreme Court's Obamacare opinions) is unhelpful and misleading, even ludicrous. A mandate requiring us to carry medical insurance bears little resemblance to being required to simply 'buy' something. On the contrary, a medical insurance mandate requires people to enter into an elaborate book-length contract with a large and powerful insurance company, and to make payments on the policy (or a substitute) in perpetuity. The present and future price of the compulsory contract is unregulated and beyond the consumer's control. The other terms of the contract are also non-negotiable. The best consumers can hope for is a menu of policy options to choose from, which will generally not include alternative medical practices and traditions. Much of the country even lacks multiple competing insurers. In short, the mandate is nothing like having to buy broccoli or get a health club membership.

It is more like a very plausible future scenario I've raised before, requirements that those of us with dependents carry life, accident or mortgage insurance. Such mandates could easily be rationalized: Social Security survivor benefits are insufficient, and uncertain going forward; and the social costs and dislocation resulting from an accident or untimely death of an income-earning family member can be catastrophic. Clearly, these and other forms of insurance mandates are closely analogous to the medical insurance mandate, and permissible under the Supreme Court's ruling. As with most public policy, including Obamacare, judicial tests for behavioral mandates would seek merely a rational basis (any plausible governmental purpose) for the legislation, instead of using heightened or strict scrutiny (considering a law constitutionally suspect unless a compelling government need, that is not otherwise accomplishable, can be demonstrated). Many types of actions (or inactions) could be coerced on pain of taxation using this low judicial standard.

WHY NOT USE TAXATION TO COMPEL US TO VOTE?

Government's future use of a new or latent power can be difficult for us to imagine. Let's take a real-life example of a government requiring its citizens to vote. We don't do that, but many countries do, including some we truly respect, like Australia. A plausible reason (rational basis) for requiring people to vote is that our participation in elections is so low, our democracy is threatened by lack of involvement. There are plenty of counterarguments, but the point is that there are plausible arguments either way. Australians aren't daft.

So imagine that Congress invokes its powers under Article I, Section 4, and passes a law compelling us to vote in congressional elections, or suffer a penalty. Imagine also that the Supreme Court strikes down the law for reasons analogous to its aversion to the Commerce Clause regulating inactivity. In the case of compulsory voting, the Justices might rule that Congress may regulate "the manner of holding elections," that is, how the voting process occurs, but that power over "manner" does not extend to forcing people to vote. Just as government may regulate the manner in which we drive our cars, but it may not force us to drive.

Sigh of relief. Government can't force us to vote.

Not so fast. In the same ruling, the Justices allow that the government may tax us for not voting, under the Taxing and Spending Clause, even if they have no express enumerated power to compel voting. They use the same reasoning as in the Obamacare decision. Under the new law, after you vote you save your ballot stub and send the IRS a copy, or pay a tax. Sound impossible? Not anymore.

The correct constitutional response to the compulsory voting law, as it should have been in the case of Obamacare, is that government may not tax us for failure to do something, because government has no delegated power to compel us to do it. To do otherwise, the Court should rule in such cases, is a violation of the Tenth Amendment. If a power is "not delegated to the United States by the Constitution," as the Tenth Amendment states, that power is "reserved to the states respectively, or to the people." Otherwise, any time the federal government lacks an express power – whether to require us to carry medical or other types of insurance, or vote, or even have a health club membership and buy broccoli – it can get around the Tenth Amendment by using taxation to coerce the behavior.

IT GETS WORSE: THE FIRST AMENDMENT TRUMPED BY THE TAXING POWER

To put the exclamation point on this reductio ad absurdum – to underscore the constitutional absurdity of a federal power to tax behavior the government cannot otherwise regulate – let's imagine a different principal argument in the imaginary compulsory voting case before the Supreme Court.

One of the objections to compulsory voting surrounds the notion that voting is a form of speech, and so also is non-voting (maybe expressing disapproval of the political system, or the process, or the candidates themselves). In this case the argument against compulsory voting doesn't center on an interpretation of Article I, Section 4, but on First Amendment freedom of speech rights. Compulsory voting, by this argument, is compulsory speech. And let's suppose that the Court agrees: compulsory voting would violate free speech rights.

Sigh of relief. Government can't force us to vote.

Not so fast. In this second hypothetical, analogous to the rulings in the first hypothetical and Obamacare, the Court finds that the government can still tax people for not voting, even though compulsory voting violates the First Amendment. In this case, imagine that the Justices employed a strict scrutiny test, but found a clear and present danger to democracy from the degree of lack of participation.

How could that be possible? Well, if the Court can ignore the Tenth Amendment, and allow Congress to tax behavior it has no power to otherwise regulate, it can equally ignore the First Amendment by a similar, if heightened, reasoning. Despite its relative disuse, the Tenth Amendment is not the poor cousin to the more famous First. Our Bill of Rights does not imply a hierarchy. In fact, it could be argued that the Tenth is ultimately more important, as it articulates the principle that the federal government's powers are limited to those delegated by the Constitution, and that remaining powers are reserved to the states and people. It's a fundamental statement of divided powers and sovereignty. So if Congress can tax behavior while violating the Tenth Amendment, why not the First?

Bottom line: we open a Pandora's Box to the federal government, if we mistakenly concede that it has constitutional authority to use taxation to regulate behavior.

December 16, 2010
CAN GOVERNMENT REQUIRE US TO PURCHASE HEALTH INSURANCE?

The universal mandate of the new federal health care law is being widely challenged, and for obvious reasons. The Commerce Clause ("Congress shall have power...to regulate commerce...among the several states") doesn't justify the mandate, because our federal laws specify that health care insurance is a state-by-state business. If I want to move from California to Hawaii, I don't just submit a change-of-address form to Kaiser. I have to quit Kaiser here and re-apply over there. Health insurance by federal definition is not interstate commerce.

Following that line of reasoning, it would then be OK for a state--but not the feds--to pass a law requiring its residents to purchase health insurance. But that doesn't sound right, and I think we all know in our bones there is something very odd about the whole idea, whether we support the new health care law or not. The justification given for a universal purchase mandate (among other reasons) is that since insurers can't turn applicants away any more, why wouldn't people wait until they're sick before getting health insurance? If that were to happen, premiums on people with health insurance would skyrocket. The healthy insured would end up paying for the unhealthy uninsured, like we do now, only worse.

So we are all required to purchase a service at an unregulated price. There are rather few health insurance companies to choose from in any state. In some states certain providers have a virtual monopoly. So all of us are required to purchase a necessarily expensive insurance product at an unregulated price from a very large corporation that may have a market almost all to itself? Laws prohibiting a person from paying directly for his or her health care services, with cash or credit card, à la carte, as needed?

The same reasoning behind a health insurance mandate could be used to require us to purchase life insurance. Breadwinners who die unexpectedly often leave their families financially destitute. We all pay indirectly from the resulting social dislocation: welfare, food stamps, homelessness, school dropouts, drugs, crime, etc. So should we then require everyone in our society with dependents--like spouses or children or grandparents--to purchase life insurance? From a handful of large corporations offering life insurance policies at unregulated prices?

Clearly no level of government, state or federal, should be allowed to require people to purchase insurance as a condition of living. If you want to own a boat, or airplane, or car, we can reasonably require liability insurance as a condition of use. But the purchase of health insurance, merely because you're alive and breathing, and living in the U.S.A.?

Let's cut to the chase: is there anything in our Constitution that prohibits state governments from making us buy something? Short answer: No, but there should be. The closest we can come is the Contracts Clause ("No State shall...pass any...Law impairing the Obligation of Contracts"). That provision – largely observed in the breach – is designed to keep governments from excusing its favorites their contractual obligations. A broader Contracts Clause should prohibit government from intrusion in private contracts generally, either to excuse parties' obligations or require a person's entering into a contract. And if you think buying health insurance is not participation in a contract, wait until you see the forms you have to fill out and sign....

March 14, 2011

A REQUIREMENT TO MARRY, THE CONSTITUTION, AND THE INDIVIDUAL MANDATE

I read a statistic not long ago that approximately half the marriages worldwide are arranged. Is that accurate? No matter. Obviously countless millions of marriages are still arranged, which is to say, compelled, and many societies and legal systems across the globe smile on such arrangements.

Let's try to imagine – with great difficulty – that some type of requirement to marry were instituted in this country, at either the state or federal level, such that if you didn't comply, you would be financially penalized by the government.

Suppose the policy arose because of some great disease that wiped out much of the population, so we needed to compel survivors to marry and hopefully procreate. Perhaps, more mundanely, society decided it would be more cohesive, with a tighter social fabric and less indigence, if people were required to marry and thus encouraged to care for one another. Maybe society would decide to require males and females who cause a pregnancy to marry, to ensure they care for the child. Imagine a misguided policy directed toward protecting Native American or Hawaiian populations, whose societies and peoples have been decimated by our prior actions: perhaps their cultures and bloodlines will dilute or die off if they are not required to marry among themselves.

Any such requirements to marry would of course be repugnant to us. If laws like that were ever passed, we would expect them to be promptly shot down in court as unconstitutional. But what part of the Constitution would we cite to put an end to such madness? Not a simple question to answer.

Our higher judicial authority, especially the Supreme Court, has a history of thrashing around a bit to cite reasons to strike down odd, clearly unacceptable law. Maybe they would find a First Amendment freedom of expression right, or a broad freedom of association, to disallow requirements to marry. They might find the proper prohibition in the Fourth Amendment, with an implied right of privacy, that makes who you marry, or whether you marry, your own personal business. Maybe they would cite the Fourteenth Amendment, protecting our right to liberty, and the protections of due process. A requirement to marry, they might aver, by its very nature is a violation of due process of law, and would therefore be an unconstitutional deprivation of our liberty. If all else fails, there is always the Ninth Amendment, which reminds us that there are rights the Constitution doesn't mention, which are still rights that we retain, mention or no.

I believe the real reason we would find any requirement to marry repugnant is because we retain, in our cultural bones, the right to freely enter into a contract, or in this case, to freely not enter into a contract. It is such an obvious right that it is not mentioned in the Constitution, yet our legal system recognizes that any contract not entered into freely, is not in fact a legally binding or valid contract. This is a venerable common law understanding. Marriage is of course a term contract (the term being the shared lifetimes of the spouses). Although there is no passel of paperwork attendant to a wedding – unlike a real estate transaction – anyone who has undergone a divorce can confirm that a marriage is indeed a very complicated contract.

What does this have to do with the new legal requirement that we all purchase a medical insurance policy, also a very complicated contract? Many arguments are surfacing for and against the universal purchase mandate, usually focusing on the federal aspect of the question: whether it is a legitimate regulation of interstate commerce by Congress; or if a legitimate political goal of Congress, like facilitating decent health care for all, inherently justifies the means chosen to achieve that end.

Federal concerns miss the basic point, because none of the legal repugnance is removed if the purchase requirement occurs at the state, not the national, level. It really doesn't matter what level of government issues the purchase requirement. It would equally violate your right to freedom from unwilling contract, whether it came from Washington, or your state house, or your county or city or suburb or town or village.